NEVER
GIVE UP!

NEVER
GIVE UP!

Relentless Determination to
Overcome Life's Challenges

JOYCE MEYER

New York   Boston   Nashville

FaithWords
Hachette Book Group
237 Park Avenue
New York, NY 10017

www.faithwords.com

Printed in the United States of America

Originally published in hardcover by Faithwords.

First Trade Edition: November 2010

10 9 8 7 6 5 4 3 2 1

FaithWords is a division of Hachette Book Group, Inc.
The FaithWords name and logo are trademarks
of Hachette Book Group, Inc.

The Library of Congress has cataloged the hardcover edition as follows:

Meyer, Joyce
Never give up : relentless determination to overcome life's
challenges / Joyce Meyer. — 1st ed.
p. cm.
ISBN: 978-0-446-58035-9
1. Success—Religious aspects—Christianity.   2. Christian life.
3. Determination (Personality trait)   I. Title.
BV4598.3.M47 2008
248.4—dc22
2008016200

ISBN 978-0-446-56401-4 (pbk.)

CONTENTS

INTRODUCTION

More than anything else, I want you to know you can have a deep, intimate, personal relationship with God through Jesus Christ and the very best life has to offer. God is no respecter of persons (see Acts 10:34) and His promises apply equally to everyone. Yes, you can have the very best God offers, but you will have to be determined to never give up until you have succeeded in every area of life.

I believe God has a great purpose for you, and I urge you to not settle for anything less. He wants to bless you and give you a life that will not only thrill you, fulfill you, and bring you deep joy and sweet satisfaction but also challenge you, stretch you, frustrate you at times, and even lead you to moments when you are tempted to give up.

Think of this book as a manual to use as you pursue the best in every area of your life. It will give you the inspiration you need to keep putting one foot in front of the other when you grow weary on your journey and remind you over and over again, in a variety of ways: *You can do it if you never give up.* It will give you strength to soar above life's tests and trials like a majestic eagle, increase your determination, and teach you how to turn adversities into opportunities. It will empower you to persevere, and build your confidence in God's ability to see you through to the achievement of the goals He has given you. It will strengthen your faith in His desire to fulfill the dreams He has put in your heart.

As you walk through the pages of this book, you will become acquainted with amazing people, people who refused to settle for less than the best and whose stories will inspire you and astound you. With every word you read, I will be cheering you on, reminding you God is on your side, and urging you to never give up.

One of the primary reasons people give up is that they try things, don't succeed, and feel like "a failure." The truth is that we are never a failure unless we give up. When we don't succeed at something, many times we do not have the courage to try again, and we settle for less than we could achieve or enjoy if we would simply keep trying. The fact is, we all have times when things just don't work out the way we hope they will, even though we do our best. We may fail at one thing, or even a few things, but that certainly does not make us a failure in life. I believe these temporary setbacks are part of life and we must experience them in order for us to ever be truly successful. Failing at some things on our way to success humbles us and teaches us lessons we need to learn. For people who never give up, failure is simply the fuel for greater determination and success in the future.

Some of the most successful people in history failed and, instead of being discouraged, refused to give up. For example, consider the following:

- Henry Ford, who invented the automobile, went broke five times before he succeeded in business.
- The great dancer and movie star Fred Astaire took a screen test at MGM studios in 1933. A studio memo reported he was slightly bald, could not act, and could dance a little.
- The family of Louisa May Alcott, the great author who wrote the popular book *Little Women,* thought she should abandon the idea of being a writer and become a seamstress instead.
- A newspaper fired Walt Disney for lack of ideas, and he went bankrupt several times before building Disneyland.
- Enrico Caruso's parents believed a voice teacher who said he had no future in music—he simply could not sing at all. He did not believe the teacher and became one of the most famous opera singers in the world.

- Theodore Roosevelt suffered the deaths of both his mother and his wife on the same day in 1884 before he became a war hero and a very effective president of the United States.
- John Wesley, the founder of Methodism, was often asked to not return to churches after preaching in them once. When he preached on the streets, townspeople kicked him out. When he preached in a meadow, people turned a bull loose on him. But later, because he refused to give up, he preached in a pasture and ten thousand people came to hear him.

The story of Abraham Lincoln also amazes me. In the face of many defeats, he had reason to believe there was no way he could succeed in life or be president of the United States. At twenty-two years old, he failed in business. One year later, he ran for the legislature and lost. When he was twenty-four, he experienced a second business failure. At twenty-six, the woman he loved passed away, and he suffered a nervous breakdown the next year. When he was twenty-nine, he lost another political race, and at thirty-four he made an unsuccessful run for Congress. At thirty-seven, he did get elected to Congress, only to be defeated again two years later. At forty-six, he lost his bid for the Senate, and the next year, he failed in his attempt to become vice president. When he was forty-nine, he was defeated for the Senate again. He had four sons, but only one lived to adulthood. But, at fifty-one years of age, Abraham Lincoln was elected president of the United States, and successfully led the country through one of its most difficult periods. Many people would have said, "No way," but not Lincoln. He never gave up.

In addition to the well-known people who had to persevere, there have been countless others whose names we do not know, but whose failures or mistakes became some of the best-known, best-selling products in the world today.

For example, Ivory soap was never intended to float. It floats because of a manufacturing error—and its buoyancy is the quality that distinguishes it from every other soap on the market.

Similarly, the material used to manufacture Kleenex tissues was originally intended to be used to make filters in gas masks during World War I, but it did not work. It also failed as a cold cream remover. But when someone decided to package and market it in the form of disposable handkerchiefs... well, you know the rest of the story.

I believe you are destined to do great things. God created you for a purpose. He has opportunities He wants to give you and assignments with which He wants to entrust you. I'm sure you have realized by this point in your life that you will face opposition as you follow God. People who are called to greatness meet great challenges. He never promised us it would be easy. In fact, He guarantees us adversities in His Word. He also promises to be with us through difficulties, to fight on our behalf, to strengthen us to overcome any obstacle we confront, and to give us the ability to overcome them under one condition—that we never give up.

No matter what comes your way, *refuse to quit*. Before you get started, I want to remind you of a biblical truth to carry with you through the pages of this book and long after you finish it: "God, who got you started in this spiritual adventure, shares with us the life of his Son and our Master Jesus. *He will never give up on you. Never forget that*" (1 Corinthians 1:9 The Message, emphasis mine).

NEVER
GIVE UP!

CHAPTER 1

NEVER SAY "NO WAY"

*"Without the way, there is no going; without the truth, there
is no knowing; without the life, there is no living."*
THOMAS À KEMPIS

Have you ever faced a situation and said, "There is no way this can
ever be"? Maybe some of these thoughts weigh on your mind:

- There is no way I can handle the pressure at work.
- There is no way I can pay my bills at the end of the month.
- There is no way to save my marriage.
- There is no way my children will ever grow up to be responsible adults.
- There is no way I can keep my house clean and straight.
- There is no way for me to open my own business.
- There is no way I can go back to college at my age.
- There is no way I can lose the weight I need to lose.

I want you to know there is always a way. It may not be easy; it
may not be convenient; it may not come quickly. You may have to go
over, under, around, or through. But if you will simply keep on keeping on and refuse to give up, you *will* find a way.

I want you to make yourself a promise. Promise yourself that you will
never again say, "There is no way." The truth is, even when there seems
to be no way, with God there is always a way. If you are a born-again

Christian, the Spirit of God lives inside of you. All the creativity in the world resides in Him, and because He lives in you, you have access to all that creativity. The Holy Spirit can give you ideas that never occurred to you and show you ways to do things you never thought you could do.

Instead of dwelling on our difficulties, we need to focus more on the fact that God is for us and His power is at work in us. Often, we give up too easily, saying, "This is too hard" or "This is taking too long." We must stop looking at situations in our lives and thinking, *I really cannot handle this; it's too much for me. I've already tried too many times. I have to accept there is just no way it will ever happen.* Instead, we need to say, "I don't care whether there seems to be a way or not. Jesus is the Way; His Spirit lives in me; and I will find a way!" God promised He would make a way in the wilderness and rivers in the desert (see Isaiah 43:19).

Jesus said in John 14:6, "I am the Way and the Truth and the Life." He is the way, and He will help you find a way where there doesn't seem to be one. First Corinthians 10:13 says, "For no temptation...has overtaken you and laid hold on you that is not common to man...but with the temptation He will [always] also provide the way out (the means of escape to a landing place), that you may be capable and strong and powerful to bear up under it patiently." In other words, God always has a way for us if we will look for it, wait for it, and refuse to give up on it.

> *I wonder how many times people give up just before a breakthrough, on the very brink of success.*

I wonder how many times people give up just before a breakthrough, on the very brink of success. You can feel the same way for ten years and then suddenly, one day you wake up and everything will change. You don't feel any different than you have felt any other day. Nothing looks any different than it ever has; nothing appears to be happening, but something does happen; and when you go to bed that night, your dream has finally been fulfilled, the situation you lived in for so long is finally over, or you finally achieve the accomplishment for which you labored for years.

I know a young woman who was once working at a job she did not particularly like and was single but wanting to be married. Within one month she became engaged and was hired for her dream job. She waited for what seemed an eternity, but at the right time God made a way. God's ways are not our ways, but His way is always best!

God has a plan for you and He has heard your prayers; you may not realize how close you are to your breakthrough. Even if you have to wait three, four, or five more years, if you will keep pressing on, you *will* have the victory you need. Whatever you do, do not give up on the brink of your breakthrough. Do not stop hoping, believing, and trying. Instead, say, "I will never quit; I will never give up; I will never say, 'No way.'"

THREE KEY ISSUES

I have encountered thousands upon thousands of people over the past thirty years in ministry and I have observed that most people consider three aspects of their lives most challenging and most worth fighting for: health, finances, and family. I have dealt with each of these areas on a personal level over the years and have seen great improvements and victories. If you are willing to persevere through the struggles you face in your health, your family, and your finances, I know you will emerge victorious too.

Never Give Up on Your Health

I'm amazed by the number of people who simply do not feel strong, vibrant, and healthy. I often overhear people telling each other, "Oh, I am so tired"; or, "I would do some of the things I enjoy if I had the energy." This lethargic approach to life is not God's best for us! God wants us to feel good and have the passion and energy we need to enjoy our lives and do everything He calls us to do. He does not want us to be too exhausted or depleted to do the things that give us joy or move us forward in His purposes for our lives.

Though some people do suffer with various conditions that must be treated with medication or therapy, many health problems people struggle with are stress related. Other health conditions develop because people do not take care of themselves; they do not eat healthily, drink enough water, exercise regularly, or get enough rest. If they would simply make some lifestyle changes, their health and quality of life would improve dramatically.

In chapter 8, I discuss in further detail the ten-year period during which I struggled with various health problems. I saw many doctors during that time, and all of them told me my problems were stress related. As I learned about nutrition, exercise, living a balanced life, and reducing stress, my health improved remarkably. I feel better today than I felt thirty years ago.

My daughter Sandra has a similar testimony. She felt badly and suffered with health problems for years. Many of her problems resulted from the stress that came with being a perfectionist's perfectionist. After she gave birth to her twins, she had terrible digestive problems, back pain, and other physical challenges to the point that she had to be taken to the emergency room several times. Sandra finally reached a point where she knew in her heart she could be healthy and feel well. She determined to find the causes of her problems and to solve them. Though she had to be diligent and disciplined, she refused to give up on the prospect of good health. As she applied the lessons she learned about nutrition and exercise, and learned how to keep the stress of perfectionism (worry, fear, etc.) from affecting her physically, she began to feel better and gain strength. Now, she feels terrific and is in good health.

I urge you to do everything you can do to improve your physical health. Make the lifestyle changes you need to make to feel better and be stronger and more energetic. If you need to change your eating habits to include more fruits and vegetables and less sugar and fat, change them. If you need to drink more water and fewer soft drinks, do so. If you need to discipline yourself to sleep a certain number of hours each night, adjust your schedule to accommodate the sleep you need. If you need to exercise more, start exercising more.

In addition, deal with the stress and emotional issues that affect you physically because your mental and emotional state certainly impacts your body. Being a perfectionist may be affecting you, as it did Sandra. Maybe worry is causing your blood pressure to be higher than it should, or perhaps fear or nervousness is affecting your digestive system. Maybe stress and tension are giving you headaches or causing your muscles to stay tight instead of limber. No matter what is affecting you, make sure you seek help for it so it does not make you feel bad or do permanent damage to your body.

If you are tired, lethargic, or simply not feeling well, see your doctor. Find out why you do not feel well and learn what to do about it. Do not settle for poor health when good health is just a few lifestyle changes away. Do everything you can do to feel well and be energetic.

Never Give Up on Your Finances

So many people are trapped in debt these days, struggling to pay their bills at the end of each month, wondering how to build a savings account, and concerned about how to finance their retirement or their children's education.

I remember when Dave and I had to buy clothes for our children at garage sales and drive cars so old we never knew if they would run or not. In the early days of our ministry, we could not afford to stay in hotels when I preached meetings at night, so no matter where we were or how tired we were, we had to drive home. Sometimes we were so exhausted we had to pull over on the side of the road to sleep for several hours before we could continue. I can remember buying canned goods with no labels because they were on sale at the grocery store. I never knew whether I would open those cans to find peaches, green beans, alphabet soup, or cat food, but the "mystery cans" were so inexpensive I had to try them.

I share these memories to let you know I understand financial hardship. I also know from personal experience, and from seeing God turn around the financial situations of countless others, that you should never give up on your finances. Never allow yourself to believe you will always be in debt or never be able to save money.

Bookstores and libraries are full of resources designed to help you break free from the bondage of debt and become a wise steward of your money. With discipline, determination, good counsel, and enough time, you can eliminate your debt, pay cash for your purchases, make investments, and save for the future. Do not think financial freedom is not possible for you, because it is. It may not be easy, but you can achieve it.

Never Give Up on Those You Love

Before Dave and I married, he asked God to send him someone he could help. When God sent him me, he got more than he bargained for! Because of the abuse in my background, I had serious, serious problems. Trying to be in an intimate relationship with me would have been extremely difficult for anyone, and I am sure many men would have given up. But Dave continued to pray and seek God for ways to help me, even when I acted as though I did not want help. At times, he even wept because he did not know what to do. He has even shared that he often went for a drive in the car to pray and cry, and returned home trusting that God would change me. After a few days, he noticed I had suddenly changed. I had not totally changed, but at least he saw progress and that let him know God was working.

I am so thankful today that God was faithful to Dave and to me. He had to lead me along an arduous path of healing, deliverance, and wholeness. He had to teach me to think differently, to trust people, to allow myself to be loved, and how to love others. He even had to teach me to be nice because I grew up thinking I had to protect myself, which meant I was often defensive and harsh.

Our journey was not easy, but Dave refused to give up on me, and we both refused to give up on God. Now we have had more than forty years of marriage, and I can honestly say our relationship is better than ever. Though our early years were difficult, we have had many years of happiness and we look forward to many more.

Like Dave, I also had the opportunity to refuse to give up on someone I loved. My oldest son, David, and I were so much alike we could hardly stand each other at times. At one point, he worked in the ministry and the two of us clashed so intensely I finally decided to tell him to find another job. I did not want to fire him, but I did not believe I could endure the conflict that characterized our relationship. I planned to talk to him and let him know his presence in the ministry simply was not working, but God spoke to my heart, *Don't give up on David.*

Over time, David and I learned to get along well. Now he runs our world missions department, has opened eighteen foreign offices for us, and oversees numerous international outreaches. I am very thankful for his good work and glad God told me to not give up on him.

When you are tempted to give up on your loved ones, remember David and me. Dave refused to give up on me, and I refused to give up on David. Whether you are believing for someone you love to become a Christian, change their behavior, leave a bad relationship, stop using drugs, go back to school, come home, or get a job, keep believing change is possible. Do not give up on the ones you love; your patient love and faithfulness may be exactly what they need to make a complete turnaround.

Love never fails. In other words, it never gives up on people. The apostle Paul describes what love is in 1 Corinthians 13 and mentions that love always believes the best; it is positive and filled with faith and hope. While Jesus was on earth, He gave a new commandment to His followers: that we love one another (see John 13:34). I believe walking in love should be the main goal of every Christian.

God is love (see 1 John 4:8) and He never gives up on us. Let's choose to live with that same attitude. Believe in the power of love to change and transform anything and anyone.

AGAINST ALL ODDS

When I think of people who never gave up, I think of my friend Pennie Sheperd. Her story is the remarkable account of a woman who experienced a tremendous miracle of God's grace and healing in her life because she was determined to reach her goal.

When Pennie Sheperd was thirteen years old, she fell and broke her tailbone. For years after that accident, she lived in chronic pain. When she got out of bed each morning, she felt as though someone had jammed a knife into her back. After she married, there were times her husband had to help her out of bed. She could not stand or sit for long periods of time or bend over to wash her hair in a sink. She slept with an ice pack, or a heating pad, or lots of pillows, but nothing seemed to help. She exhausted every possible avenue of escape from her agony. At times, she was almost completely overwhelmed; at other times, she was depressed by it and thought, *How can I live through one more day?*

Pennie's doctor, Caroline Rogers, diagnosed her with post-trauma arthritis and degenerative disc disease. This caused muscle imbalances, which led to problems in parts of her body where she had not suffered previously. She was trapped in a cycle of pain and suffering that was irreversible—unless, of course, a miracle happened.

Pennie loved God and truly believed He could heal her. She believed every day held the potential for a miraculous healing in her life. So day after day, year after year, she asked God for her miracle.

As Pennie prayed one day, she heard these words in her heart: *Run to your miracle.* Those words did not make sense to Pennie, because she was not a runner and had never been one. She didn't like to run, and she lived in so much pain she did not even want to try. But when God spoke to her heart, *Run to your miracle*, she committed to do so.

The greatest distance she could think of running was a full-length marathon—26.2 miles! So with her family's support and her doctor's permission and offer to act as her trainer, she began the grueling physical and mental training process.

For the next four months, Pennie pushed through the pain to train for the marathon. She kept a strict diet and a rigorous schedule seven days a week, eventually getting up by 3:00 a.m. to get in a long run before a full day of work and family responsibilities. After several months of training, Pennie had no relief from her pain, so she continued to pray about her participation in the marathon to make sure the pain was not an indicator she should stop training. She was determined to pay the price of progress and to not give up. She wanted to be able to stand at the starting line and know she had done everything God asked her to do.

The day of the marathon drew near, but just two weeks before the race, her knee went out. The night before the race, she could hardly walk around her hotel room. She still believed God had spoken to her and felt she had to press through the agony. She was determined to show up at that starting line. She said, "I am going to the starting line even if someone has to carry me to get me there."

Her husband and daughters, her strongest supporters, wrote scriptures and inspiring messages all over her hands and arms. Before sunrise on marathon day, she literally hobbled up to the starting line, with Dr. Rogers beside her, knowing she was exactly where she was supposed to be. She was going to run to her miracle!

As she stood at the line barely able to walk, she turned to Dr. Rogers and cried, "My back doesn't hurt! My back doesn't hurt!" She had not said those words for twenty-eight years. Her knee hurt like crazy, but her back didn't hurt!

Dr. Rogers suggested they begin the race by walking to warm up and see how the knee responded. About a mile and a half into the race, Pennie told Dr. Rogers, "I think I'm going to be able to run."

Throughout the whole race, she had much encouragement. A group of friends prayed for her during the seven hours of the race. Her husband and daughters were at the starting line and at regular checkpoints along the way to encourage and support her.

At the fourteen-mile marker, Dr. Rogers and Pennie were thirty-six seconds off the seven-hour pace, which meant a "sweeper" would pick them up and drive them to the finish line if they did not make up the time. But Pennie gave it her all.

At the twenty-three-mile marker, she hurt so badly her daughters began to run with her—one under each arm to help support her. Pennie crossed the finish line in about seven hours.

On our *Enjoying Everyday Life* broadcast, she said, "Before the race, I had always envisioned in my mind that I would cross the finish line and get my miracle. The truth is, I was not healed at the finish line; I did not receive my miracle at the finish line. I got my miracle at the *starting* line. All I had to do was show up. It doesn't take running a marathon to get a miracle. In my case, it took obedience and commitment."

Pennie Sheperd is a woman who could have said, "No way." Instead, with God's help, the support of family and friends, and a "never say no way" attitude, she never gave up. Pennie's miracle took place in January 2004 and she is still healed today.

GET A GOAL

Right now, I want you to think of an area in your life in which you need to refuse to give up. Come up with a goal—one that will require you to be disciplined and to overcome some obstacles, but one that promises great reward. It may be as basic as making your bed each morning, or as ambitious as running a marathon or climbing Mt. Everest. It may be to break free from a fear of flying or a fear of public

> *Get with God and decide what your goal needs to be and what is worth putting your energy into.*

speaking, or it may be to overcome a physical handicap or a learning disability. It may be cleaning your house or getting out of debt.

If other people think your objective is too easy, then that is too bad. If it is a legitimate goal for you, then stick with it. If other people think it is impossible, do not allow them to discourage you. Just make sure you and God are in agreement and then go after your goal with everything in you.

You will see as you read this book that rewards await those who overcome. I am praying that God will help you be full of "holy determination"—not some kind of fleshly determination or willpower—but true God-given determination. I encourage you to pray and be determined to be disciplined and diligent in every area of your life, because that is the way you will overcome your obstacles and enjoy your hard-won successes. Take life one day at a time and remember that God has rewards in store for you. Don't you dare miss them!

BE SMART ABOUT IT

Many people never accomplish their goals because they do not know how to set them. A popular and easy-to-remember acronym that has been successful in helping countless people reach their goals is the word *smart*:

Specific
Measurable
Attainable
Realistic
Timely

Let me elaborate.

Specific: Make sure your goal is as specific and accurate as possible. For instance, don't simply say, "I want to lose weight"; say, "I want to lose ten pounds in the next three months. Every time you hear yourself speaking of your goals in vague terms, ask yourself, "What does that mean?" You'll soon find yourself making comments such as, "I am going to stop watching television at nine-thirty every night and be in bed by ten" instead of, "I need to watch less television and get more sleep."

Measurable: Goals that are hard to measure are goals that are hard to meet. Before you commit to a goal, decide how you will monitor your progress. For goals involving debt reduction, you can measure your progress with monthly statements. For goals that involve exercise, you can keep track of how many pounds you can lift or how many miles you can run. Whatever your goals are, find ways to measure them, whether that includes a journal, a checklist, a chart, a graph, a spreadsheet, or some other creative way to see how you are doing.

Attainable: Make sure the goal itself is reachable. Don't have a goal of losing thirty pounds in one week or paying off all your debt in one year—when your debt is more than your annual salary. Choose goals that lie just beyond your reach—not so easy that they don't challenge you, but not so difficult that they stretch you to the breaking point.

Realistic: I believe in dreaming big dreams and aiming high, but don't set yourself up for disappointment by trying to reach an unrealistic goal. Assess all the factors that will affect your ability to reach your goals and work within those parameters. Make sure it is realistic, given your health and physical condition, finances, schedule, personal capacity, and other priorities.

Timely: People who set goals without target completion dates rarely accomplish their objectives. Give yourself deadlines by which to accomplish your goals. If you are working toward a goal over a long period of time, consider setting intermediate goals each week or month, to keep you on track.

He Coined the Phrase

You may know of him as one of the most effective political leaders ever to stand on the world stage or as one of the most highly regarded statesmen of all time, but do you know what former British prime minister Winston Churchill suffered before he ever achieved greatness?

Winston Leonard Spencer Churchill's premature birth occurred on November 30, 1874—two months before he was due. He was born into a prominent English family, but his parents had no time for him. His mother did not feed him, but left him in the care of a wet nurse when he was an infant, and with a nanny as he grew older, while she pursued social activities. His father, a busy political leader, never demonstrated much interest in him.

Churchill had a difficult life, certainly one full of challenges, tumult, opposition, and near misses. His parents sent the neglected boy to boarding school as a child. He did not excel academically (except in English and history) or socially. He had a speech impediment (which he never completely lost) and failed to make friends or even get along well with others. Later in life, he told stories about having to dodge cricket balls his fellow students threw at him. After that, at age nineteen, he nearly drowned in an accident in Lake Lausanne, and much later at age fifty-seven, he was hit by a car in New York City.

A graduate of the Royal Military College, the short, stocky, shy Churchill served in the British army as a young man. During that time, he saw combat; participated in a cavalry charge; traveled Europe, Africa, Cuba, and India; and wrote newspaper reports and books.

At age twenty-four, Churchill resigned his military commission to pursue journalism and politics. He sought a seat in

(continued)

Parliament, but lost the election. He then traveled to South Africa as a journalist covering the Boer War, but was captured and thrown into prison. However, he managed to escape, which positioned him as a military hero upon his return to England in 1900. That same year, he ran for Parliament again, and won his seat by a narrow margin.

In 1940, Churchill became prime minister, and in that position, exercised brilliant, courageous, strategic leadership that rescued Great Britain from the edge of seemingly certain defeat to victory in World War II.

In 1941, while visiting the school where he had studied as a youngster, the then–prime minister Churchill is erroneously reported to have given a three-word speech: "Never give in" and then promptly returned to his seat. In reality, Churchill gave a longer speech which included these words: "This is the lesson: never give in, never give in, never, never, never, never—in nothing, great or small, large or petty—never give in except to convictions of honor and good sense. Never yield to force; never yield to the apparently overwhelming might of the enemy."

I encourage you today as Churchill exhorted the schoolboys in 1941: "Whatever you do, *never* give in—and never, never, never give up."

CHAPTER 2

NEVER GIVE UP ON YOURSELF

"By perseverance the snail reached the ark."
CHARLES HADDON SPURGEON

A farmer once took an egg from an eagle's nest. He took it home and placed it under one of his hens and it hatched with a little brood of chickens. The farmer raised the bird with great patience and attempted to tame him. The eagle never really seemed to fit in with the chickens. It always walked alone; it could not seem to relate to or interact with the chickens.

As the eagle grew, he realized something seemed to be wrong deep inside of him. Even though he had never known any other existence but life in the chicken yard, it just did not feel like home to him. He wanted to leave the chicken yard and take to the skies. He even tried to do so, and the farmer finally had to clip the eagle's wings to keep him from flying away.

Since the eagle could not fly, he just sat in the chicken yard looking up at the sky. One day a storm began to brew, the sky grew dark, and all the barnyard animals scurried around for cover; the chickens were terribly frightened, as chickens are prone to be. The eagle sat watching the scene in front of him, realizing the storm did not frighten him in the least.

At that moment, he could not help but stretch out his wings, and as he did, he noticed that the farmer had failed to keep them clipped.

Suddenly, his eye caught sight of a great eagle riding the wind above him, his wings outstretched in majestic form.

The eagle that was raised as a chicken looked again at the chickens scurrying around frantically, then returned his gaze to the eagle soaring peacefully above him, then looked back at the chickens and then up at the eagle again. He heard the eagle let out an awesome, piercing cry. In that instant, he knew he had to get out of that chicken yard! A mighty gust of wind swept beneath his outstretched wings and lifted him into the air. With a shrill scream of victory and freedom, he left the barnyard forever.

YOU HAVE THE HEART OF AN EAGLE

I wanted to share the story of the eagle in the chicken yard with you to fill you with a fresh sense of encouragement to never give up on yourself. I hope it stirs something deep inside of you—something that makes you want to press through every obstacle you face, to be who you are, and to make the courageous choices needed to break free from everything holding you back from the greatness for which you were created.

> *Do you ever feel you are like an eagle in a chicken yard? You know there is much more within you than you are experiencing and expressing in your life right now.*

Do you ever feel you are like an eagle in a chicken yard? You know there is much more within you than you are experiencing and expressing in your life right now. You know God has a great purpose for your life—and you cannot escape or ignore the inner urge to "go for it." But do you also know you will have to work hard; take risks; endure loneliness; leave some things behind; make some difficult decisions; or perhaps be misunderstood, judged, or even criticized in order to achieve and enjoy the fullness of God's destiny for your life?

Know this: All eagles are uncomfortable in a barnyard. They all long for the clear, blue, open skies. When you are living in a place that keeps you from being who you were made to be and doing what you are meant to do, you will be uncomfortable too. When the thought of moving beyond where you are begins to take root in your heart and mind, when a seed of greatness begins to grow, when you have a burning desire to step out of where you are or a desire to be adventurous and do something new or different, pay attention to it. Begin to act on it. But also realize that people around you may not understand your desire to break out of the box. They may want to clip your wings. They may even say, "Now just settle down and be like all the other chickens. Here you have this nice chicken yard and these nice little worms and grubs. Why should you ever want any more than that?"

When you hear such comments and questions, something inside of you may ask, *What is wrong with me? Why do I think as I think? Why do I feel this way? Why can't I just settle down and live a normal life like everybody else?* The reason you cannot just settle down is that you are not a chicken; you are an eagle! You will *never* feel at home in that chicken yard because you were made for something bigger, more beautiful, and more fulfilling.

I encourage you today to fan the flame inside of you. Fan it until it burns brightly. Never give up on the greatness for which you were created, never try to hide your uniqueness, and never feel you cannot do what you believe you were made to do. Realize your hunger for adventure is God-given; wanting to try something new is a wonderful desire; and embracing life and aiming high is what you were made for. You are an eagle!

LIKE AN EAGLE

The eagle is one of nature's best examples of strength, perseverance, and determination. It is a bird who refuses to be denied its destiny, one who never gives up. As you and I continue on our journeys through life and stay committed to never giving up, we can learn some important lessons from this powerful, majestic bird.

Eagles and chickens have one characteristic in common: they are both birds. Aside from that, they could not be more different! I have spoken many times about the fact that different kinds of birds often remind me of the different types of Christians I have observed in the body of Christ. Certain characteristics of these birds are similar to characteristics of some people, and I believe, by the time you read about them, you will see what I mean.

The Chicken

First, I think about chickens. Chickens are generally skittish and afraid of life; they are lazy; and they rarely reach their potential. Chickens simply scratch around barnyards and cluck. We do not see chickens flying, because chickens flap; they do not fly. They need to live inside the confines of a fence and are satisfied to do so. They cannot handle freedom; they must be kept in a chicken yard. As you read in the story at the beginning of this chapter, when a storm comes, the chickens' first response is to flap around in the chicken yard, stirring up dirt, and to run to the chicken house to huddle in fear with all the other chickens, trying to find a little grub worm on the way.

Christians who "flap around" and "run for the chicken house" when difficulties arise are not living the victorious life Jesus died to give us. We have to stop running from things, especially the storms in life. We are more than conquerors (see Romans 8:37). We can be confident in God at all times, and we can stay peaceful in the midst of storms. God has called and equipped us to *overcome,* not to be fearful or intimidated.

The Magpie

Magpies are overly aggressive bullies who abuse other birds. "Magpie Christians" generally drive others away from God and are selfish, arrogant, and self-centered to the point of rudeness. These harsh, pushy Christians cause much disrespect toward the kingdom of God and give fellow believers a bad name.

The Kookaburra

To the kookaburra, life is one big party, one big joke. "Kookaburra Christians" are those who take nothing seriously and laugh at everything (even when laughter is totally inappropriate). They are not sensitive to anything around them and they often wound, hurt, and offend others.

The Bible says we need to be sober-minded (see 1 Peter 1:13). That does not mean we can't have fun, but it does mean we need to pay attention to what is going on around us; be sensitive; and understand there are times when certain stories, jokes, or types of behavior are appropriate and times when they are not.

The Vulture

We know vultures, or buzzards, as the garbage collectors of the bird kingdom. They are drawn to death and uncleanness. These birds enjoy destruction and the filth of life—everything corrupt, rotten, and stinking.

"Vulture Christians" are attracted to people with problems. They love to see people suffer and fail, and they use their words to destroy people's lives. They spread rumors and seem to secretly enjoy ruining the reputation of a person or ministry.

Parrots and Cockatoos

Parrots and cockatoos are the "talkers" in the bird kingdom. "Parrot Christians" are those who "talk the talk," but do not "walk the walk." They appear to know much more than they do because they have learned to repeat what they hear and to mimic what others say. They may have some intellectual knowledge of God, but no personal relationship with Him. They are all noise and no action, all talk and no depth of experience.

The Cuckoo

Cuckoos do not like to work and are happy to sponge off other people. These birds will not even build their own nests; they look for nests other birds have already built, lay their eggs there, and then leave their babies for other birds to raise!

Regrettably, there are cuckoos in the church today. They exist on handouts; they do not want to work. Sometimes they are not even born again, but they operate under a religious spirit. They want to ride on the coattails of other people's faith and enjoy the benefits of the Christian life without investing in it.

The Peacock

If you have ever seen a peacock, you know they strut around as though they own the entire world. "Peacock Christians" are flashy, showy, overly ambitious, worldly, full of pride, and very much in love with and impressed with themselves. They have large egos and feel superior to everyone else. They love to "strut their stuff"—clothes, cars, jewelry, and other things—but are selfish and have little or nothing for people in need.

The Pelican

The big, jolly pelican has a big mouth and is only interested in eating. He seeks whatever he can find to fill his belly.

"Pelican Christians" do the same. They have ravenous appetites and hunger for the Word of God. They could become spiritual giants, but are content to sit on the couch eating junk food, watching television, and ignoring their spiritual lives. They are always happy to let others take positions of spiritual leadership, even though they could do so if they would simply put forth a little effort.

The Canary

Canaries and other caged birds are usually beautiful birds with tremendous potential who spend their lives locked in cages. They do not seem to realize the bondage in which they live; they even sing in the midst of it!

"Canary Christians" are those who go merrily along, either oblivious to or content with the "cages" they live in. Perhaps they are trapped in religious tradition, a lifeless church, a powerless prayer life, inferiority or insecurity, or a host of other problems that keep them from enjoying the freedom and joy available to them in God. They refuse to break free; therefore they never embrace life in all its fullness.

The Crow

If you have ever visited a farm or read a story about one, you know that some fields have scarecrows. The crows must be scared away because they damage the crops. These dirty, noisy animals eat what does not belong to them, reducing the value of a farmer's livelihood and spoiling the fruit of his labors. Crows also enjoy destroying the young of other species. They are cunning, dangerous, and only out for themselves. Nothing matters except their own selfish desires, and they seek their own fulfillment ravenously.

"Crow Christians" also enjoy hurting others and causing destruction. They think nothing of ruining a pastor's reputation or dividing a church. They are some of the most cunning and dangerous people in the church.

One interesting fact about crows is they spend a great deal of time pestering eagles. If you want to be an "eagle Christian," which I will write about in the next section, get ready to be pestered by the crows in the kingdom.

The Eagle

In the midst of all other birds, we find the eagle. Bold, strong, courageous, fiercely devoted the eagle has many wonderful characteristics. Charles Prestwich Scott rightly observed, "Eagles come in all shapes and sizes, but you will recognize them chiefly by their attitudes." Among its other admirable traits, an eagle is loyal and committed, a reliable mate, and a devoted parent. An eagle has sharp, keen eyesight and knows how to fly efficiently by riding the thermal currents of the earth. This bird dwells on the rocks in high places and is confident enough to fly alone and to stand alone in life when necessary and to be strong against the storms, spreading its wings and soaring above the clouds and storms of destruction.

EAGLES OR CHICKENS?

Over the years, I have encountered many people who are eagles but think they are chickens. That is a real problem because eagles who think they are chickens will act like chickens. They will scratch and flap around the barnyard making noise instead of soaring confidently and smoothly above the storms beneath them. The Bible tells us a powerful truth about our thoughts: "As he thinks in his heart, so is he" (Proverbs 23:7). In other words, we become what we think. The things we think about, focus on, and surround ourselves with will shape the people we become. If a bird thinks he is a chicken, he will be fearful and go into hysterics when a storm comes, but if he thinks he is an eagle, he will be strong and courageous.

Let me ask you some important questions, and I really want you to ponder them and answer them honestly: What do you think of yourself? How do you feel about yourself? What is your attitude toward yourself? Do you respect yourself? Do you value yourself?

You have a relationship with yourself. You are with yourself more than you are with anybody else; you can never get away from yourself. You cannot ever go anywhere in the world without yourself, no matter how hard you try. This is why valuing yourself, liking yourself, and feeling good about who you are is so important.

Many cultures in the world suffer from a self-respect crisis, and I think one reason for it is that people don't take care of themselves because they don't value themselves enough. Some even believe putting themselves at the bottom of their priority lists is holy! They think God wants them to neglect their own well-being and just sacrifice... sacrifice... sacrifice and serve everyone else.

Yes, we are called to sacrifice, to serve others, to give, and to not live greedy, self-centered lives. At the same time, we are also called to realize and embrace the truth that we are the people in whom God dwells. We belong to Him; He wants to use us; He wants us to be the kind of people who cause others to want to know Him—and to do these things, we must value and take care of ourselves.

You are God's house (see 1 Corinthians 6:19). You are His building, His temple, and He lives in you! You will destroy the temple by being overcommitted, overworked, living on junk food, not drinking enough water, not getting enough sleep and rest, and failing to exercise. In that condition, you cannot be much good to yourself, to the people around you, or to God because you will not be healthy and energized. You will not be able to persevere through difficult times in life or to fully enjoy the good times.

I urge you today: start respecting yourself and taking care of yourself mentally, physically, emotionally, and spiritually. Discipline yourself to get enough rest, to eat healthily, to stay hydrated, and to exercise. You will be surprised how your mind changes, your emotions settle, and your body feels strong and healthy. To get started on this healthy lifestyle, let me recommend my book *Look Great, Feel Great*.

I believe you are created to be an eagle. God wants you to be an "eagle Christian," one who can fly high, be bold, live with power, keep circumstances and relationships in perspective, live at peace, stay strong, and soar above the storms of life. Begin to see yourself that way, because that's the way God sees you. Begin to value yourself, because He values you. Walk out of any "chicken mentality" you may have, and live like the eagle you were created to be.

DON'T GIVE UP WHEN YOU ARE ALONE

Most of us, when we think of an eagle soaring, envision a lone bird flying majestically against a bright blue sky. We don't think of eagles in pairs or in flocks. This is because eagles soar alone. They do not fly in flocks, as geese do, or in a covey, as quail do. In the United States, you can watch a congregation of swallows leave San Juan Capistrano, California, every October and then watch them return in March. These birds migrate south for the winter together and make a "group trip" back to California each spring. You might happen upon a bevy of larks, chirping or singing together, but you will not come across a bevy of eagles. They simply do not travel in groups. Something about the character, the strength, and the nature of the eagle gives it the courage to soar by itself.

The first lesson we need to learn if we want to be "eagle Christians" is that we will have to fly alone at times. This does not mean we cannot have relationships or be friends with people. It simply means we will often have to make and act upon decisions that separate us from the pack and enable us to reach higher heights than the people around us may want to go.

One time, I was complaining about being lonely: "I don't have any friends. I seem to spend all of my time alone. Everybody thinks I'm strange and different; they call me a fanatic. Some people in my family don't even like me anymore..." The Spirit of God spoke to my heart: *Just remember this: other birds fly in flocks, but eagles fly alone. What do you want to be, Joyce?*

If you are going to be an "eagle Christian," you may go through some lonely seasons in life. There may be times when you have to go it alone—perhaps as a parent or at work—and follow your convictions in spite of peer pressure. Maybe it's as small as being tempted to tell a white lie to your boss or succumbing to the pressure to "fudge the numbers." As parents, we are often called to stand alone in the best interests of our children. All of your son's friends may be allowed to play video games that you believe are too violent or to surf the Internet without supervision. It is not easy to take a stand against the opposition or your colleagues—and it's even harder when it's your unhappy child!

Maybe it's as simple as being the only one who does not attend a function or do something others are doing. For example, you might have to stay home and spend an evening with God while all your friends go to a party.

Going to the party may not be wrong in itself, but if you are going to be an eagle, you may have to skip the party because you feel you are tired and you know you need to rest. You may be a bit grouchy and realize that you need to spend some quality time with God so you can get your attitude renewed.

In all of these cases, you may have to take a stand and not be overly concerned about what people think or say. Setting limits with your children or with colleagues may be the harder choice. Spending the evening alone praying and studying God's Word may not seem exciting to your emotions. But in both cases, you and those you love will reap the benefits of wisdom and stability. You will also have the peace of knowing you obeyed God instead of merely doing what you felt like doing.

I need to spend the first couple of hours every day with God, because if I don't, I could be grumpy and short with people. But I want to be an eagle for God, so I take time with Him at the beginning of every day. This is what Isaiah 40:31 means when it encourages us to wait for God.

Being an eagle doesn't mean you will never be weary or feel stressed; it means you run to God and allow Him to renew your strength when you do feel weary or pressured. Many of us could avoid losing our tempers or saying words we later regret if we would simply spend some extra time with God when we realize weariness is setting in. This will help you keep going strong and not want to give up on yourself.

Don't stop short of knowing who you are, valuing who you are, and encouraging yourself to be and do everything God intends for you. Even when you feel like an eagle surrounded by chickens, don't quit believing in God's purpose for your life, and never give up on yourself. You may be well aware of your weaknesses, but don't be discouraged by them. Instead of allowing them to separate you from God, run to Him with them. He is the only One who can help you overcome them. We all have faults and flaws, so don't give up because of yours. Remember, God is not surprised by your faults. He knew about them before you did—and He loves you anyway!

Noble and Nobel

Marie Curie, also known as "Madame Curie," was the first woman to ever win a Nobel Prize—and she won two of them, a truly remarkable achievement.

Born Maria Sklodowska in Poland in 1867 to a piano player and a mathematics and physics professor, Marie demonstrated an interest in education at an early age and won academic awards for her school achievements and acclaim for her remarkable memory. She hoped to continue her education following her completion of secondary school at age sixteen, but her father lost much of his money through an unwise investment; so Marie had to go to work as a teacher, dashing her hopes for further study—at least temporarily. When she was eighteen, she took a job as a governess, during which time she endured a sad love affair.

Marie and her sister Bronia, both affected by their father's loss of money, agreed that Marie would use the earnings from her governess job to finance Bronia's education; and when her education was complete, Bronia would fund Marie's studies. Both sisters kept their promise to each other.

Marie traveled to Paris in 1891 to further her education in mathematics, physics, and chemistry at the world-famous university, the Sorbonne. With amazing dedication, Marie lived in a small, cramped student-housing facility, where she survived primarily on bread, butter, and tea.

At the Sorbonne, Marie met physics professor Pierre Curie, and the two married in Paris in 1895. Marie and Pierre committed their lives to science, particularly to the study of radium and polonium, which they isolated in 1898 and Marie named in honor of her native country. Though their research was brilliant,

(continued)

they had to conduct it in its early years under very poor laboratory conditions and were unable to support themselves with their work, so Pierre and Marie both had to spend hours teaching in order to make a living and provide for their two daughters.

Marie's findings earned her a doctorate in 1903, the same year she, Pierre, and Antoine Henri Becquerel received the Nobel Prize for physics. In 1904, she was able to leave her job as a physics teacher at a nearby girls' school and become the chief assistant in Pierre's laboratory. The couple worked diligently and intensely, and among other significant achievements, discovered radioactivity.

The couple's successful scientific partnership came to a tragic end in 1906, when Pierre was hit by a car and killed. Though his death had a profound impact on Marie, it also intensified her resolve to carry on the work the couple had begun. She was soon appointed to fill the teaching position her husband had held, professor of general physics in the faculty of sciences, and thereby became the first woman to teach in the Sorbonne.

In 1911, Marie Curie won a second Nobel Prize, this time for chemistry, and continued in her dedication to her work, particularly in finding therapeutic uses for radium in an attempt to apply it in medical situations to alleviate human suffering.

Marie Curie could have given up on her desire to pursue her education, decided not to suffer through the difficult laboratory arrangements under which she worked, and given up on her work in the wake of her husband's death. But she pressed through her challenges, delays, and difficulties—and contributed greatly to scientific advances that continue to affect and save lives today.

CHAPTER 3

REFUSE TO LIVE IN FEAR

"The only thing we have to fear is fear itself—nameless, unreasoning, unjustified terror which paralyzes needed efforts to convert retreat into advance."

FRANKLIN D. ROOSEVELT

The first African American licensed aviator was a beautiful, vivacious, and courageous young woman named Bessie Coleman, who came to be known as "Queen Bess." She was also the first American woman to earn an international pilot's license. Before she accomplished these remarkable achievements, Coleman dreamed of adventure in her hometown of Atlanta, Texas. When she was twenty-three years old, she finally ventured outside the confines of small-town life and moved to the big city of Chicago to be near several of her brothers and to pursue a life that had been beyond her reach in Atlanta, Texas.

In Chicago, Coleman worked as a manicurist in a barber shop, where she listened to stories about World War I pilots and their adventures in the sky. She dreamed of becoming a pilot herself, but could not afford to do so. At the barbershop, Coleman met two influential businessmen who wanted to help fund her training. One was a newspaper man who thought her story would be good for business. Because flight schools in America did not train black women, Coleman studied diligently to learn French and moved to Paris to attend flight school in 1920. Upon her return to America, she gained much media attention, and people of all races embraced her as they learned about her in the newspapers. Throughout her career, she participated in air shows and was invited to attend important events.

Bessie Coleman died in a plane crash, probably resulting from a wrench in one of the gears, on April 30, 1926. More than ten thousand people attended the funeral of this courageous young woman who refused to give up.

Bessie Coleman faced much discouragement and many obstacles because American flight schools refused to accept her and she had to put her dreams on hold while making the effort involved in learning a foreign language. She had to move alone to a new country, which took great boldness for the determined young woman. Even though her path to success was not as easy as those of her white counterparts, she found a way to do what she really wanted. It required extra time and effort, but she did not let fear or the uncertainties of moving to a foreign country keep her from pursuing her dream—because she was determined to not give up.

NO NEED TO FEAR

For many years, well-known advice columnist Ann Landers typically received approximately ten thousand letters per month, most of which had to do with people's problems and struggles. When asked what she thought was the biggest problem in people's lives, she responded with one word: fear.

Indeed, many of us struggle with fear. Let me begin by saying those of us who are believers in Jesus Christ have no need to fear. He is always with us. He loves us with a perfect love, and as 1 John 4:18 says: "There is no fear in love [dread does not exist], but full-grown (complete, perfect) love turns fear out of doors and expels every trace of terror!"

God knows the minute He calls us to do anything big or small that will take us to a new level—change careers, get married, have children, leave behind all that's familiar for a life on the mission field, go back to work after twenty years as a homemaker, get serious about diet and exercise—the first emotion that typically hits us is fear. Whether it's low-level nervousness or full-blown panic, most of us experience some degree of fear when we think of doing something new. Our minds are filled with excitement, yet we think, *What if this? What if that? What if? What if? What if?*

NEW LEVEL, NEW DEVIL

Any time we step out to do something new, especially something new for God, we will almost always—and almost immediately—face a negative circumstance that will try to discourage us or convince us we cannot do what God asks of us. Something will come up to tell us it is too hard; it does not make sense; it will not work; or we are not qualified to do it. The enemy uses such words and thoughts to discourage us, hoping fervently we will never accomplish what we set out to do.

Revelation 12:4 gives insight on how the devil tries to plant fear in us before we even get started. It says, "And the dragon stationed himself in front of the woman who was about to be delivered, so that he might devour her child as soon as she brought it forth." The woman mentioned in this verse was about to give birth, but the dragon (who represents Satan) had stationed himself in front of her so he could devour her newborn child.

This scene represents a dynamic that often happens in our lives as believers. Every time God puts a fresh, new idea in our hearts or gives us a dream, a vision, or a new challenge for our lives, the enemy will be there to oppose us. I am not referring simply to the times we want to do "big" things for God; the enemy is not selective. We face new levels often. When we receive Jesus as our Savior, that's a new level. When we begin to move into a deeper walk with

God, or begin to pray bolder prayers, those are new levels. When we begin to give time, money, and energy into God's kingdom, we are moving to a new level. God constantly calls us to new levels; some seem big and important, while others may seem relatively small or insignificant. Whatever the case, when we reach a new level, we face a new level of opposition from our enemy, the devil. The Bible tells us that opposition comes with opportunity (see 1 Corinthians 16:9), but God is always with us and we have no need to fear. Some things may seem too great for us, but nothing is impossible with God. He is not surprised or frightened by anything.

If we are going to do anything great for God and if we are determined never to give up on our dreams, we have to take chances; we have to be courageous. When we face situations that threaten or intimidate, we do not need to pray so much for the fear to go away as we need to pray for boldness and a courageous spirit. I can promise you, fear will not go away. It is not something we can get rid of, so we must learn to overcome it.

The spirit of fear will always try to keep us from going forward. For centuries, the enemy has used fear to try to stop people, and he is not going to change his strategy now. But we can defeat fear; we are more than conquerors through Him who loves us (see Romans 8:37). Courage is not the absence of fear; it is pressing forward while the feeling of fear is present.

THE RIGHT PERSPECTIVE ON FEAR

I teach often on Isaiah 41:10 because it encourages us and helps us know what to do when we are afraid. "Fear not [there is nothing to fear], for I am with you; do not look around you in terror and be dismayed, for I am your God. I will strengthen and harden you to difficulties, yes, I will help you; yes, I will hold you up and retain you with My [victorious] right hand of rightness and justice."

What does this scripture mean when it says, "Fear not...for I am with you;...I will strengthen and harden you to difficulties"? It means God makes us stronger and stronger as we go through things. It also means that over time, we become less affected by the difficulties and challenges we face. It is like exercise. When we first do it we get sore, but as we press through the soreness we build muscle and gain strength. We must go through the pain to get the gain.

Consider your life. Are there situations you now handle well that would have previously made you feel fearful and anxious? Of course there are. As you have been walking with God, He has been strengthening you and hardening you to difficulties. In the same way, I can also assure you and encourage you that some of the things bothering you right now will not affect you the same way in five years. I often feel fear when I do certain things for the first time. But after gaining some experience, that feeling is no longer present. We must press through feelings and never allow them to control us.

> *If God removed all fear, we would never grow and overcome obstacles.*

If God removed all fear, we would never grow and overcome obstacles. He often permits difficulty in our lives because He is trying to reveal something that needs to be strengthened or changed in us. Our weaknesses are never revealed in good times, but they quickly show up in times of trial and tribulation. Sometimes He shows us what we are afraid of because He wants to deliver us from that fear and strengthen us for things that will come in the future. In those times, we need to say, "Thank You, God, for allowing me to see that fear in my life. It reveals an area that needs to be dealt with in me." Once that particular area of fear is dealt with, then the enemy will have a very hard time bothering you—and succeeding— in that area again. This is one way God hardens us to difficulties and teaches us to not be afraid.

No matter what we may go through in life, we must always remember that God only does us good as long as we live (see Deuteronomy

8:16). Some things may not feel good initially, but they will work out for our good if we keep going forward and trust God each step of the way.

GOD SAYS, "I WILL BE WITH YOU"

The presence of God in our lives helps us overcome fear. If we know by faith that God is with us, we can take on any challenge with confidence and courage. We may not always feel God's presence, but we can trust His Word and remember that He said He would never leave us or forsake us (see Deuteronomy 31:6).

In Joshua 1:1–3, God called Joshua to a great challenge of leadership—taking the children of Israel into the Promised Land: "After the death of Moses the servant of the Lord, the Lord said to Joshua son of Nun, Moses' minister, Moses My servant is dead. So now arise [take his place], go over this Jordan, you and all this people, into the land which I am giving to them, the Israelites. Every place upon which the sole of your foot shall tread, that have I given to you, as I promised Moses."

The Bible simply tells us in this passage Moses had died and Joshua was going to take his place as the leader of God's people. As soon as God gave this news to Joshua, He immediately assured him: "No man shall be able to stand before you all the days of your life. As I was with Moses, so I will be with you; I will not fail you or forsake you. Be strong (confident) and of good courage" (vv. 5–6). Later in this same scene, God encouraged Joshua again, saying, "Be strong, vigorous, and very courageous. Be not afraid, neither be dismayed, for the Lord your God is with you wherever you go" (v. 9). Basically, God was saying to Joshua, "You have a big job to do, but don't let it intimidate you. Fear not. Do not be afraid because I will be with you."

In the Bible, the basis for not fearing is simply this: God is with us. And if we know God's character and nature, we know He is trustworthy. We do not have to know what He is going to do; simply knowing He is with us is more than enough.

Fear is a spirit that produces feelings. When God told Joshua to not be afraid, He was not commanding him to not "feel" fear; He was commanding Him to not *give in* to the fear he was facing. Perhaps you have heard my teaching, "Do it afraid." That basically means, when fear attacks you, you need to go ahead and do whatever God is telling you to do anyway. You may do it with your knees knocking or your palms sweating, but do it anyway. That's what it means to "fear not."

When I feel afraid I often meditate on scripture because it strengthens me to keep pressing forward, no matter how I feel. The Word of God has power inherent in it and will actually strengthen you on the inside. I have personally been encouraged quite often by Genesis 28:15: "And behold, I am with you and will keep (watch over you with care, take notice of) you wherever you may go, and I will bring you back to this land; for I will not leave you until I have done all of which I have told you."

Every man or woman who has ever been given the opportunity to do something great has had to face fear. What will you do when you are tempted to be afraid? Will you run, or will you stand firm, knowing God is with you?

FACING FEAR

One meaning of the word *fear* is "to take flight," so when we use the phrase "fear not," in a very real sense we are saying, "Don't run away from what frightens you. Face the situation; don't run from it. Don't try to hide from it; just meet it head on, even when you'd rather not."

One of the women who works at Joyce Meyer Ministries has a remarkable testimony. When faced with a life-threatening illness, she decided to not run from her fear. She was very fearful when she received her diagnosis, but she did not give up—she pressed through. It is my hope you will find encouragement to face your fears, whatever they may be, with God's empowerment until you see victory, just like Peggy did. Here's how she tells it.

After forty-eight years of living my life "my way," I found myself in the emergency room at a local hospital. My sisters took me there because they were concerned about the way I looked. I was pale; I had trouble sitting up; and I had shortness of breath because my abdomen was enlarged. On March 2, 1996, I was diagnosed with ovarian cancer.

I went through the surgery, a complete hysterectomy (during which surgeons removed a twelve-pound tumor), and then after a four-week recovery from the surgery I took chemotherapy treatments for six months.

When I first heard my diagnosis, I was naturally very scared; I thought I was going to die. The cancer was in late stage three, and I felt I had been handed a death sentence. My doctors were very concerned, and one of them told me some women live five to ten years after surgery and chemo. This was not all that encouraging to me, and it was then I decided to begin praying and evaluating my life. As is the case for so many people, it took a serious wake-up call to get my attention.

I attended church as a child (mostly Sunday school), and I did believe in God. Not long after I began praying, I noticed I had a sense of peace, and I developed a good attitude about my situation. It was hard to explain to my friends and family, but I knew I would be fine if I did not give up hope.

My chemo treatments ended in October 1996. I was put on disability and informed I could not work for at least five years. During one of my many follow-up visits to doctors, one asked if he could pray with me in his office; I said yes. He

suggested a church for me to go to. I went three times and on
the third time I received Jesus as my Lord and Savior! That
was on March 2, 1997. Exactly one year to the day I had been
given the "death sentence," I received eternal life! I have been
serving God ever since, and I am completely cancer free!

Peggy learned to face her fear of death by turning her life over to
Jesus Christ. As she did, she was healed and she learned a valuable
lesson: running away from fear does not work, but courageously facing it with God's help brings hope and victory.

I also had a bout with cancer in 1989. I went to the doctor for a
routine checkup and was told two days later that I had breast cancer and needed to have a quick mastectomy because the tumor they
found was a very aggressive form of cancer. To say I was shocked
and frightened would be an understatement, but God quickly
reminded me of His Word and gave me courage to go forward. I actually thought of just ignoring it and going on with my life. (People
often do that, you know, because it's a way of running from the problem rather than dealing with it. They just ignore things hoping they
will go away. The problem is: those things don't go away.) Had God
told me to not have surgery, I wouldn't have, but I actually felt in my
heart that I was to have the operation, so I did. Like Peggy, I heard
all the negative reports about the possibility the cancer could return.
But that was nineteen years ago, and I am still cancer-free.

One young woman had a different kind of brush with death, but like
Peggy, she never let the odds against her survival keep her from keeping
on. Like most recent graduates, Juliane Koepcke must have been filled
with excitement after graduating high school. The German native had
finished her studies in Lima, Peru, where her father worked as a biolo-
gist. Juliane and her mother were seated side-by-side on a flight that
would take them from Lima to join her father in Pucallpa.

When the plane carrying ninety-two people flew into an unex-
pected storm, Juliane noticed the right wing outside her window seat

in flames. Her mother commented, "This is the end of everything." The next thing Juliane knew—and the last thing she remembers— she was tumbling through the air, still strapped to her seat.

Several hours later, Juliane awoke somewhere in the vast Amazon rain forest unable to see out of one eye and having suffered a broken collarbone and a deep cut in her arm. After releasing herself from her seat, she began searching for her mother. She found nothing more than some empty seats and the bodies of three young women. Juliane soon realized she was the only one who survived the crash.

Juliane was determined not to die in the rain forest, but had no idea where she was and no one to help her. In her traumatized state, she somehow remembered hearing her father say that a downhill direction in a jungle always leads to water, and water always leads to civilization. So she struck out alone, moving downhill all the way, bushwhacking her way through the rain forest. She heard planes overhead, but could not signal them from beneath the thick growth of the Amazon.

After ten grueling days, Juliane finally saw a small hut and found salt and kerosene inside—exactly what she needed to get the worms out of her skin. On the eleventh day after the crash, she met a group of hunters from Peru, and they took her to an airport where she was able to catch a plane to meet her father. Juliane refused to give up for eleven agonizing days, never knowing what she would face in the jungle. She went on to become a zoologist based in Germany.

THE FEAR OF FAILURE

The fear of death is just one of many fears we may have. The truth is, we have all kinds of fears—everything from fear of heights to fear of spiders to fear of public speaking. In the remainder of this chapter, I want to talk about a different kind of fear that affects the core of our beings—the fear of failure.

There are many reasons why the fear of failure gets a stranglehold on us. It could be rooted in the fear of what other people think of us.

We do not want others to think negatively of us, or maybe we do not want to live with bad thoughts about ourselves so we don't even try to do things, thinking we are protecting ourselves from feelings of failure. Whatever the case, the fear of failure can be so strong that it can keep us from stepping out and taking on challenges and risks.

If you want to be a courageous person who never gives up, you need to squarely face this kind of fear. Fear of failure will keep you from going to the next level in your life, or it will prevent you from even taking the first step toward your goal. It will hold you back from doing and being everything God has for you if you do not confront and conquer it. Always remember, when you take steps to face your fear of failure and deal with it: God is with you! Also, remember that people never fail unless they stop trying. When we do make mistakes along the way, we can always learn from them and allow them to add wisdom to our lives. We can "fail forward"!

What Is It?

The fear of failure is crippling because it holds people back from acting on their desires, and it will certainly hinder you from fulfilling your destiny. The fear of failure is nothing more than the fear we will be unable to do what needs to be done in a specific situation. In other words, we will not succeed at something we attempt to do. This fear is especially active in us when we think of doing something we have never done before. We are afraid we will fail, so we fail to try. When I look at my own capabilities apart from God, I am afraid of everything, but if I keep my eyes on Him I am assured that *through Him* I can do whatever He asks me to do (see Philippians 4:13).

CREATED FOR ADVENTURE

The truth is, we were never created to do the same things all of our lives. God has put a craving for adventure in us, and adventure means trying something we have never done before. Adventure means stepping out, doing something different, doing something a little bit on the edge, and not always living in a zone that we consider "safe."

I assure you, if you are supposed to do something, God will make you able to do it. You do not have to *feel* able, and you do not have to have experience. All you need is a right motive and a heart full of faith. God is not looking for ability; He is looking for availability. He is looking for somebody to say, "Here I am, God, send me. Here I am, use me. I want to serve You, God. I want to do something for You!"

I remember a particular Sunday in my church many years ago. That day I had to confront a dreadful fear of failure that could have kept me from going deeper with God. At that time of my life, I truly loved God, but there were so many biblical truths and principles I did not know. I knew a little bit about what a person needed to do to be saved, but I did not understand victory, overcoming obstacles, power, authority, or being used by God. I had no real hope that my life would ever be any better than it was at the time.

In that church, we had missions Sunday once a year, and on that day, we always sang the song "Here Am I, Send Me." I remember one specific time, something welled up in me from the bottom of my heart and I sang the words with every fiber of my being: "God, here I am! Send me! Send me!" I do not know where I thought He would send me because I had a husband and three small children; I was abused as a child and spent my time simply trying to survive every day. But in my heart, I sensed I wanted Him to use me. I may not have had a lot of ability, but I was available to God. I was willing to say, "I may fall flat on my face, God, but if You want to use me, I am willing to try."

If you want God to use you, do not let the fear of failure stop you from obeying Him as He leads you. God not only sees where you are, He sees where you can be. He not only sees what you have done, He sees what you will do with His help.

Following God is often like walking in a fog. We can only see one or two steps in front of us, but as we take those steps the next ones become clear. With God, we do not always see clearly ahead into the distant future, but if we are willing to trust Him we will have an exciting journey that will make life adventurous and worth living.

Failure or Stepping-Stone?

No one sets out to fail or wants to fail. But as I wrote in the introduction to this book, I do believe "failure" can be an important stepping-stone on the way to success. Failure certainly teaches us what *not* to do, which is often as important as knowing what we *are* to do! So-called failure is all about how we look at it.

Many stories have circulated about how many times Thomas Edison failed before he invented the incandescent light bulb. I have heard he tried seven hundred times, two thousand times, six thousand times, and ten thousand times. No matter how many attempts he made, the number is staggering. But he never gave up. Edison is reported to have said in all his efforts he never failed—not once; he just had to go through many, many steps to get it right! It takes that kind of determination if you are really going to do anything worthwhile.

The man who led IBM to worldwide prominence, former president Thomas J. Watson, had no fear of failure. In fact, he had this to say about it: "Would you like me to give you a formula for success? It's quite simple, really. Double your rate of failure. You are thinking of failure as the enemy of success. But it isn't at all. You can be discouraged by failure—or you can learn from it. So go ahead and make mistakes. Make all you can. Because, remember, that's where you will find success."

Giving in to the fear of failure will surely keep you from reaching your full potential in life. The good news is, you have no reason to fear failure. First of all, God is with you. And secondly, there is no such thing as failure if you simply refuse to quit.

Every time you are tempted to fear, remember God is with you. He will not fail you or forsake you. He is your God; He will help you and hold you in His hand. He is hardening you to be able to face difficulties. He is building in you the strength, stability, and character you need to press through to the good things He has in store for you, and He is building in you the courage to never give up.

I have often pondered why some people do great things with their lives while others do little or nothing at all. I know that the outcome of our lives is dependent not only upon God but also upon something in us. Each of us must decide if we will reach down deep inside and find the courage to press past fear, mistakes, mistreatment at the hands of others, seeming injustices, and all the challenges life presents. This is not something anyone else can do for us; we must do it ourselves.

I want to encourage you to take responsibility for your life and its outcome. What will you do with what God has given you? Are you going to invest your talent and time or hide it because of fear? I truly believe God gives everyone equal opportunity. He said, "I have set before you life and death...choose life" (Deuteronomy 30:19). *Fear is in the category of death, faith and progress fills us with life.* It is your choice, and I believe you will make the right one!

Wired for Success

Alexander Graham Bell, inventor of the telephone and founder of the Bell Telephone Company was smart, curious, hardworking, and persistent. These qualities contributed greatly to the success he enjoyed as a result of his inventions, but the real impetus behind his great inventions was the simple fact that he wanted to help people who lived with challenges and difficulties.

Bell's mother, Eliza Grace, was hearing impaired, and he wanted to find a more effective way to communicate with her than through her ear tube, as other people did. Instead, Bell spoke to her by placing his mouth close to her forehead, believing she could sense the sound waves from his resonant voice. His mother's deafness and his father's work in speech pathology and lifelong interest in helping the hearing impaired communicate gave Bell an interest in helping people communicate too.

A native of Scotland, Bell traveled to London to pursue university studies. While in England, his two brothers contracted tuberculosis and died. Bell also contracted the dreaded disease, and in an attempt to save his life, his parents moved themselves and their last remaining son to Canada. Even though his time at the University of London was cut short, it was there that he became interested in the work of a German physicist named Hermann von Helmholtz. Bell could not read German, but did not let that stop him from finding ways to learn what Helmholtz taught. One of his assertions, which captured Bell's attention, was that electrical tuning forks and resonators could be used to make vowel sounds. Without sufficient training in German, Bell misinterpreted Helmholtz's theory and thought the physicist believed sound could be transmitted over a wire, which he

(continued)

eventually accomplished. Speaking of this erroneous interpretation, he later said, "It gave me confidence. If I had been able to read German, I might never have begun my experiments in electricity." Those experiments in electricity, of course, led to the invention of the telephone.

Bell is best known as the inventor of the telephone, but he also invented several other important devices including a precursor to the iron lung used to help polio patients in the 1950s. This apparatus, too, came about as a result of personal hardship in Bell's life. In 1881, his newborn son Edward died of respiratory failure. In response, Bell designed a metal jacket that would help those with respiratory problems breathe easier. That same year, United States president James A. Garfield was shot and Bell used his abilities to try to save his life by quickly cobbling together a metal-detecting device to find the location of the bullet. Though the president died of his wounds, Bell did his best to help save him.

Let me encourage you to be like Alexander Graham Bell and let the hardships you experience and observe inspire you to be creative. Never give up as you seek to make the world a better place and to improve the lives of those around you.

CHAPTER 4

CONFRONTING YOUR FEARS

"Put an eagle in a cage and it will bite the bars,
whether they be of iron or gold."

IBSEN

Chickens often stay in the same chicken yard for their entire lives, but eagles learn to fly to new heights. As you continue on your journey toward being an eagle Christian, I want to call your attention to seven fears you must deal with in life. If you do not deal with these fears, they can keep you in the chicken yard, but as you confront them and overcome them, you will be well on your way to becoming an eagle. Never give up; face your fears with God's help and leave the "chicken mentality" behind!

SEVEN FEARS YOU MUST CONFRONT

1. Fear of What People Think

If you want to break free from where you are now and move to the next level in life, the first thing you must deal with is the fear of what people think. So many of our decisions are made to please people, not to please God. We fail to follow our hearts, but we live to please people around us because we want their acceptance and approval. We want them to like us; we want to be part of the group; we don't want them to judge us, criticize us, or speak negatively about us.

The apostle Paul dealt with this issue in Galatians 1:10: "If I were still seeking popularity with men, I should not be a bond servant of Christ." In other words, had he chosen to care about what people thought of him or sought to be popular, he could not have served the Lord the way he did. The same may be true in your life.

Wanting to please people is a fairly natural desire, but if you are out of balance and have an excessive need for people's approval, the devil can use that to steal your destiny. You will never be all God wants you to be if your goal is to please people.

I discovered that the people in my life who didn't want to make a full commitment to serving God tried to keep me from doing so. People usually try to get us to do what they are doing, rather than giving us the freedom to make our own choices. We must not give in to their pressure because eventually each of us will stand before God and give an account of our lives. We won't answer to people; we will answer to God, so we should live to please Him and Him alone.

I believe you really want to go on with God; you have a hunger to go deeper in Him; you want to be an eagle. But to do that, you will have to take the chance that some of your friends or co-workers may not understand you. Let's face it: reading your Bible during your lunch break or taking a walk and praying instead of gossiping may not be popular behavior in the environment where you live or work. People may ridicule you, but the reason for this is that your good choices cause them to feel convicted. They may call you "holier than thou" or say you have become a religious fanatic who thinks you are better than everybody else. They may reject you or speak unkindly about you, but if you know your heart's desire is simply to love God and serve Him with your whole heart, then keep pressing forward and don't let anything stop you.

As I mentioned, most of the time, the people who are upset with you for wanting to move on with God are those who do not want to go on with Him themselves. As soon as you find one other Christian who shares the same values you have and wants to participate in the same activities in which you participate, you have a new friend. God is faithful. When you want to go on in Him, He will give you new friends and surround you with people who are like-minded. I cannot promise you will not have to go through some lonely times first, but I do know God will provide the friends and companionship you need. I have certainly been through lonely times in my life; if you feel lonely, don't be discouraged because things will eventually change.

John 12:42–43 depicts a very sad situation, one that characterizes so many people's lives.

And yet [in spite of all this] many even of the leading men (the authorities and the nobles) believed and trusted in Him. But because of the Pharisees they did not confess it, for fear that [if they should acknowledge Him] they would be expelled from the synagogue; for they loved the approval and the praise and the glory that come from men [instead of and] more than the glory that comes from God. [They valued their credit with men more than their credit with God.]

The men in this passage missed having a deep relationship with God because they cared more about what people thought than about what God thought. Please don't be this way! If you struggle with the need for approval and acceptance, I encourage you to read my book *Approval Addiction.* Do whatever you must do to reach the point where you care more about what God thinks than about what your family, friends, neighbors, or colleagues think. Seek to please Him and you can soar with the eagles instead of scratching around the chicken yard with the chickens.

2.   *Fear of Criticism*

A companion to the fear of what people think about us is the fear that they will criticize us. We want the people around us to think we are smart, wonderful, and always doing the right thing. We don't like any kind of criticism or judgment, nor do we enjoy knowing someone is speaking negatively about us. We don't have to like these things, but we cannot allow ourselves to fear them.

When we suffer from self-doubt, we rely on the approval of others because that makes us feel that we're doing the right thing. Insecurity and the fear of making mistakes causes many people to make most, if not all, of their decisions based on what others think. But what makes us think that they have the answers and we don't? When we are truly confident and secure, the opinions of others cannot control us.

> *When we are truly confident and secure, the opinions of others cannot control us.*

My daughter Sandra suffered with insecurity and perfectionism for many years. I remember her asking excessively for other people's opinions and becoming very confused when they did not agree with her ideas about what she should do in certain situations. I often saw her change a decision to agree with others even though she still felt in her heart that her original decision was correct.

Thankfully, she has received healing from God in this area. Although she is very open to asking for advice, she is secure enough to ultimately do what she feels is right. She is much happier and has the peace of knowing she is following God to the best of her ability.

Many people suffer from insecurities like Sandra's and from other types of insecurity. If that includes you, I have good news: God will set you free. I encourage you to begin confronting the fear of being wrong and believe the Spirit of God lives in you to give you wisdom and to lead you in every situation.

When I think of people who overcame the fear of criticism, I think of Dr. Martin Luther King Jr. When he began to speak out against segregation and the unfair treatment African Americans received in the United States, critics came from many corners, some of them very vicious. In the face of criticism, cruelty, threats, intimidation, and imprisonment, King stayed true to his cause. When an assassin's bullet killed him on April 4, 1968, it struck a man who was determined to never give up. Because King confronted and conquered the fear of criticism, the social changes for which he labored eventually became reality and resulted in great changes in American society.

I believe anyone who does anything significant must first overcome the fear of criticism. We simply cannot follow God and keep all the people happy all the time. To do great things, we must accept that a certain percentage of people won't agree with us—and we can't let that stop us.

3. Fear of Not Pleasing God

If you want to go higher in God, you must also address the fear that your imperfections will keep you from pleasing God. This is a significant struggle for many people; they suffer terribly with secret worries that they are not pleasing to God, they are not doing enough, or they are just not doing things correctly. They're afraid God is displeased with them because they don't read the Bible enough, they don't pray properly, or they don't have enough faith. They live in bondage to the fear that nothing they do is ever enough for God. *This is a lie!* The devil wants us to believe "enough is never enough." He wants us to feel no matter what we do, God will always want something more or something different.

This is very sad, because the truth is that God isn't nearly as hard to please as we think He is! Yes, He has high standards and desires excellence in every area, but the truth is that nothing about us surprises Him. He knew what He was getting when He called us into relationship with Himself. When we make mistakes, He doesn't sit in heaven wringing His hands saying, "I am shocked by your behavior. I never expected that!" Psalm 139 tells us plainly that He knows what we are going to do before we even do it, so try to keep in mind that God knows *all* about you and loves you anyway!

Read this next statement closely: *If you could be perfect, you would not need Jesus.* Your willingness to keep pressing toward the mark of perfection is all God requires. If you are really in love with Jesus, your love for Him will keep you pressing toward perfection every day. But I can almost guarantee you will also fall short in some way every day. If you really are a sincere Christian, there is no way you can take a lighthearted, "Oh well, I don't care" attitude toward your shortcomings. Your love for Jesus will compel you to want to do better every day. You will get up the next day and try to do better again; maybe you will do better in some area, but you may fail in something else. The message God is trying to communicate to you through these situations is: "You still need Me."

> *If you could be perfect, you would not need Jesus.*

Jesus says in Matthew 5:48, "You, therefore, must be perfect [growing into complete maturity of godliness in mind and character, having reached the proper height of virtue and integrity], as your heavenly Father is perfect." When we think of being "perfect," we can feel intimidated, but we need to understand this word's meaning in its original New Testament language. The Amplified Bible makes this clear. *Perfect* means simply "growing into maturity." We need to rejoice and be happy when we are growing into maturity and stop criticizing ourselves when we are not perfect by human standards.

I want to encourage you to enjoy your journey. After all, life isn't as much about reaching our destination as it is about how we make the trip. People who struggle and are miserable all their lives but finally reach their destination don't accomplish nearly as much as those who may not arrive at their destinations, but enjoy the process.

You may have heard me say: "I'm not where I need to be, but thank God, I'm not where I used to be. I have not arrived, but I am on my way!" That kind of attitude infuriates the devil. Let me encourage you to not set a standard of worldly perfection for yourself. Instead, start getting excited about every step of progress you take. When you are not exactly where you want to be, remind yourself that neither are you where you used to be! Instead of focusing on your faults, focus on your progress. The very fact that you are reading this book shows you are making progress.

> *When you are not exactly where you want to be, remind yourself that neither are you where you used to be!*

You will have to stay focused as you confront and break the fear of not being pleasing to God. You can't allow your faults to distract you from going on with Him. He is the only One who can help you overcome your faults and weaknesses, so focus on Him instead of on them. Hebrews 12:2 teaches us a powerful lesson about staying focused: "Looking away [from all that will distract] to Jesus, Who is the Leader and the Source of our faith." The devil is the author of distraction, and he intends your distraction for your destruction. The devil wants you to be distracted because he knows if you keep your eyes on Jesus, then He becomes not only the author and source, but the finisher of your dream, your vision, and your faith.

Remember, you are no surprise to God. Your faults and failures do not catch Him off guard. He never looks at me and says, "Oh, Joyce! I didn't know you were going to be like *that!* Had I known you were going to do *that* I would not have allowed you to be a Bible teacher!" Read Psalm 139. Every day of your life was written in His book before you ever showed up on planet earth. God knows every word in your mouth, even the ones you have not spoken yet. Your shortcomings do not shock Him. He covered them at the cross with the blood of His Son.

If you really love God, if you are *in* love with Jesus, you will not want to sin or displease God. You will do everything you can to stay away from sin. But you will sin, and you cannot let that distract you or hinder you from moving on with God, because *when* you sin, you have an advocate with the Father. Jesus Christ, the all-righteous One (see 1 John 2:1), is faithful and just to forgive you for all of your sins and to cleanse you from all unrighteousness (see 1 John 1:9). Do not allow your sins, your faults, or your failures to distract you or cause you to believe you are not pleasing to God. If you are in Christ, you please Father God completely because He sees who you are in Jesus, not who you are on your own merits. Remember, we are saved by grace, not by our own works. Salvation is not the result of anything we could possibly do; it is a gift from God to be received by faith (see Ephesians 2:8–9).

4.   *Fear of Making the Wrong Decision*

In order to move forward as an eagle Christian, the fourth fear you need to deal with is the fear of making wrong decisions, which is otherwise known as self-doubt. I do not believe it is God's will for us to doubt ourselves; He wants us to have assurance and confidence.

I once made a decision a handful of people did not like; they did not think I made a good choice. There were also people who liked my decision and believed it was right. But I could not help thinking about the naysayers, and I began to wonder, *Did I do the right thing? Maybe I didn't do the right thing.* Then I talked to God about it: "Lord, did I do the right thing?" He affirmed me, saying I had made the right decision.

Just as you may have had to do, I have had to learn not to listen to self-doubt. God still reminds me from time to time to be careful in this area because Satan is always attacking us with all kinds of fears and doubts. I have learned to not merely believe my feelings, but instead to check my heart and see what I truly believe God is saying.

It is amazing what we will find in our hearts if we simply take the time to listen.

If we question ourselves excessively or carry on internal debates about whether or not we have made good decisions, we can all get lost in self-doubt and quickly become double-minded. James 1:7–8 teaches us that people who are double-minded are unstable in all their ways and should not expect to receive anything from God. Also, when we become extremely double-minded, we become confused. When we are really confused, we become discouraged and depressed. Pretty soon, we find ourselves back in the chicken yard scratching around with the chickens when we should be soaring with the eagles.

Don't allow yourself to wallow in self-doubt and become double-minded. If you think you have made a mistake, go to God about it. Say, "God, if I made a mistake, I trust You to show me. I want to know if I made a mistake or a bad decision. Please show me if I'm wrong." Then take some time, get quiet, and see what you sense in your heart. Remember, you will not hear wise direction by listening to your own mind, your emotions, or other people. *Listen to your heart!* As a Christian, the Spirit of God lives in you—in your heart—and He will lead and guide you.

Don't assume you are wrong simply because a handful of people disagree with your decision. If all the devil needs to do to get you off track is find someone to disagree with you, then he is definitely in the driver's seat where your life is concerned. Make sure you stay focused and single-minded, free from self-doubt as you continue to become an eagle Christian.

I've found that doubt often tries to visit me when I am praying. This vague feeling leaves me wondering if God is hearing me and will answer when I should be trusting that He is listening and will respond. Prayer is our greatest privilege and is necessary for God to act in the earth. The Bible tells us we have not because we ask not (see James 4:2), but it also says we must ask in faith with no wavering, hesitating, or doubting (see James 1:6). God works through our faith, not our fear. Maintaining an attitude of faith requires conscious effort on our part. We can decide to believe or doubt; the choice is up to us.

5. *Fear of Missing God*

The next fear we must confront if we are going to be determined to never give up is the fear of "missing" God, of doing something "wrong" as we try to follow Him. All I have to say is: if you miss God somehow, don't worry; He'll find you.

Part of the fear of missing God (making a wrong decision) includes the fear of deprivation. Often, when God puts a dream in our hearts and calls us to do something, one of our first questions is: "What happens if I step out and try to do this and it wasn't God's will? What if He doesn't provide for me?"

If you are afraid of missing God, all you have to do is remember how much God loves you and look at the testimonies of the people who have gone before you. The Bible is full of miraculous stories of God's guidance and provision. He is the God who caused manna to fall from the sky every day for forty years so the children of Israel would have something to eat! If you want to read more remarkable stories, libraries and bookstores carry all kinds of books that chronicle God's leading and provision for people throughout history.

One misconception Christians often have in this area is the idea that we must take upon ourselves all the responsibility of never making a mistake. In reality, the whole point of God's love and grace is that if our hearts are right toward God and we are doing the best we can, when we take a step of true faith after praying and seeking God, if we *do* make a mistake then God will help us get back on track. God has never left us, and He can make that so-called mistake somehow work out for our good. We cannot be afraid of missing God, or we will never be able to take the first step in following Him.

The truth is, everyone makes mistakes while trying to learn to follow God, but that's not the end of the world! Don't be so afraid of failing that you never try. I would actually rather try and then make a mistake than to live my life without ever attempting anything. God likes an aggressive attitude. The fear of missing God is actually the fear of failure; do not allow that fear to influence your decisions. "Step out and find out" is my motto. You cannot drive a parked car! Get going in some direction; if you make a wrong turn you can always go around the block and then head the other way.

6. Fear of Change

Former U.S. president Woodrow Wilson said: "If you want to make enemies, try to change something." For some reason, many people don't like change, and I believe it is often because they fear it.

Many times, when we grow weary or simply become bored with a situation, we get restless and begin to pray: "Oh, God! Something has to change!" Then, when God tries to bring change into our lives, we say, "Lord, what are You doing? I don't think I can take this change!" We often find ourselves caught in the tension between wanting change and fearing change.

Thank God, He never changes. Because He is always the same, we can trust Him through any changing circumstances or situations. Hebrews 13:8 says: "Jesus Christ (the Messiah) is [always] the same, yesterday, today, [yes] and forever (to the ages)." And God Himself speaks in Malachi 3:6, saying: "For I am the Lord, I do not change." This should give us great courage and comfort when we face changes in our lives. We do not need to fear change; we can handle it, because God remains the same.

What if Abraham Lincoln had been afraid of change? He would not have signed the Emancipation Proclamation and the horror of slavery would have continued in America. What if Orville and Wilbur Wright had been afraid of change? We would all be stuck with traveling on the ground or sailing over the water instead of flying through the skies. What if Thomas Edison, whom I mentioned earlier, had feared change? We would still be reading by candlelight after sundown.

I share these vignettes with you to inspire you to think about the many good changes that have made people's lives better and easier through the years. I'm sure you could make your own list of positive changes that have occurred in your life. Remember, the fear of change could keep something wonderful from taking place for you. I urge you to not let that happen, but to boldly embrace the changes that come your way.

Without change there is no growth, and anything that is not growing is dying. Change is a fact of life and the more we fear and resist it, the more we are resisting God. As I noted earlier, God Himself does not change, but He definitely changes people, circumstances, and things.

> *Change is a fact of life and the more we fear and resist it, the more we are resisting God.*

I began to notice a few years ago that the people attending our conferences were all my age or older. I started asking myself where the younger generation was and finally had to realize that I was not offering them anything to which they could relate. I determined that I would make whatever changes I needed to make in order to be relevant to the younger generation because they are the future. We can never change God's Word because it always remains the same, but we can change the way we package it and that is exactly what we did. I changed my clothing style to be in line with today's fashion. We changed the look of our conferences by adding different music styles, updated media presentation, and different lighting techniques. Although these things don't change the Word of God, which is the main thing we are trying to present, they do draw people in. By simply being willing to change some of these exterior things, we now enjoy a congregation of all ages and are delighted to see that a "generation gap" really does not have to exist if we are willing to change some of our old ways.

We all have a tendency to think according to the generation in which we were raised, but we must realize that things are always changing. If we are not willing to change, God will not stop to wait for us and we will wonder why we missed the things He is doing today.

7. Fear of Sacrifice

When we believe God is asking us to do something, we begin with the questions: *What am I going to have to give up if I do this? If I do this, what will it cost me? If I do this, how uncomfortable am I going to be?*

The truth is, anything we do for God requires an investment. Part of loving Him involves a willingness to lay our lives down for Him. Our willingness to sacrifice is part of the test He often puts us through, not so He will know if we really love Him and are serious about following Him, but to prove His love and commitment to ourselves and get it established in our own hearts.

More than thirty years ago, when God filled me with the Holy Spirit and called me into ministry, I lost almost all of my friends, was asked to leave my church, and fell out of favor with many members of my family. I was embarrassed; I was rejected; and it was difficult to press through those experiences without giving up. But it was all part of the price I had to pay to go on with God.

Do not be afraid of sacrifice when God calls you or puts a dream in your heart. Determine you will pay the price and pass the test. I assure you, it is worth it.

Fear of failure; fear of what people think; fear of criticism; fear of not pleasing God; fear of making wrong decisions; fear of missing God; fear of change; fear of sacrifice. Leave these fears in the chicken yard; they have no place in the sky with an eagle. You may be afraid to move away from your chicken yard because it means you have to leave the security of what is familiar to you. I urge you to never give up as you face your fears; spread your wings and fly with courage and boldness.

The Ultimate Overcomer

One of the best-known "overcomers" in American history would have to be Helen Keller, who refused to allow the blindness of her eyes and the deafness of her ears to keep her from enjoying her life, achieving remarkable goals, and making significant contributions to society.

Until she was nineteen months old, Helen Keller's life was relatively normal. But everything changed when she became very ill with what was then called "brain fever." Many people now believe she suffered from scarlet fever, but regardless of her diagnosis, the disease left her severely handicapped, completely destroying her ability to see and hear.

In an effort to help her, her parents took her to see Alexander Graham Bell, who gained fame as inventor of the telephone, but was also a knowledgeable teacher of the deaf and helpful resource for hearing-impaired individuals. Bell referred the Kellers to Boston's Perkins School for the Blind.

The Perkins School provided Helen with a tutor named Anne Sullivan, whom Helen affectionately called "Teacher" until Sullivan's death. As a child, Helen was extremely frustrated by her handicaps and often became violently angry. But Sullivan remained patient and diligent, and over time taught Helen to read Braille, to write, and to communicate effectively despite the fact that she was blind and deaf. To learn more about this, read the play *The Miracle Worker* by William Gibson or watch the movie by the same name.

As a young child, Helen knew she wanted to go to college and was determined not to let her handicaps deny her that privilege. After studying hard and preparing diligently, she was admitted to Radcliffe College, the women's school associated with Harvard

University, and began her studies there, with Anne Sullivan's help, in 1900. Four years later, she had mastered several languages and graduated with honors.

In college, Helen embarked on a writing career that would last half a century and include books, newspaper articles, and magazine pieces. Her first book, *The Story of My Life*, was published in 1903 and eventually found its way into print in more than fifty languages.

Before the end of her life in 1968, Helen received numerous honorary degrees and awards for her humanitarian work and the inspiration she provided for the blind and the deaf, including the prestigious Presidential Medal of Freedom. Perhaps more than that, though, she enjoyed her many opportunities to meet dignitaries such as Oliver Wendall Holmes and every U.S. president from Grover Cleveland to Lyndon Johnson.

One of the primary reasons Helen Keller never gave up on herself was that Anne Sullivan never gave up on her. Throughout this book, I have urged you to not give up on yourself, and I would encourage you in that way again now. But I also want to make sure you remember to do everything you can to inspire others to persevere through their difficulties and overcome their challenges, just as you do.

CHAPTER 5

IT'LL COST YOU!

"The block of granite which was an obstacle in the pathway of the weak becomes a stepping-stone in the pathway of the strong."
THOMAS CARLYLE

You may have heard the name Wilma Rudolph. Perhaps you know of her as an outstanding female athlete whose story was told in the television movie *Wilma* and whose image appeared on a United States postage stamp. Indeed, this phenomenal runner, coach, and sports commentator gained remarkable recognition and acclaim, but do you have any idea what it cost her to achieve her goals and live her dreams?

She was born prematurely, the twentieth of twenty-two children in a poor family reeling from the impact of the Great Depression. In addition to suffering scarlet fever and double pneumonia as an infant, she was afflicted with polio from birth and had to be driven fifty miles twice per week to a hospital for blacks, where she received treatment. In addition, her mother had to rub her legs four times each day for years. At one point, doctors told her she would never walk, but eventually she proved them wrong and walked with a brace until she was nine years old. By the time she was twelve, she could finally walk normally. Within four short years, at age sixteen, she won her first Olympic medal. Four years later, at the 1960 Olympics in Rome, she earned gold medals in three events and became an international superstar.

The little girl who was told she would never walk ended up learning to run—better than any other woman in the world. But she did not do it without pain, without sacrifice, without discipline, or without paying a price. She wanted to see her desires fulfilled—and she did because she never gave up.

To be people who never give up, we must learn to press past both natural obstacles, as Wilma Rudolph did, and unseen forces such as anger, unforgiveness, guilt, shame, and fear. Over the next several chapters, I will be writing at length about overcoming these issues so you can press through anything that is holding you back and go on to be everything God intends for you to be. Press in, press on, press through, and pay the price now so you reach your goals and your potential.

GOING THROUGH

We will all go through situations in life. Many times, we think the phrase "I'm going through something" is bad news, but if we view it properly, we realize *going* through is good; it means we are not stuck! We may be facing difficulties, but at least we are moving forward.

Isaiah 43:2 says: "When you pass through the waters, I will be with you, and through the rivers, they will not overwhelm you. When you walk through the fire, you will not be burned or scorched, nor will the flame kindle upon you." God's Word here is clear: we *will* go through things. We *will* face adversities in our lives. That's not bad news; that's reality.

Let me repeat: we will go through things in life, but the things we go through are the very circumstances, challenges, and situations that make us people who know how to overcome adversity. We do not grow or become strong during life's good times; we grow when we press through difficulties without giving up.

You may remember the tragic day in April 2007 when a gunman opened fire at Virginia Tech, senselessly killing thirty-three bright, young, promising students and himself. One of the students killed that day was Caitlin Hammaren, a vibrant sophomore and the only child of two doting parents. Caitlin's mother, Marian, had to find the will and determination to go on after such unthinkable loss.

After Caitlin's death, authorities gave her laptop to Marian and her husband Chris. They opened it and saw a note taped above the screen: "God, I know that today nothing can happen that you and I can't handle together." Marian knew Caitlin believed those words wholeheartedly, but she could not believe them for herself—not in the midst of the greatest tragedy of her life.

In the weeks and months that followed Caitlin's death, Marian struggled to make peace with her loss and find the strength to live without Caitlin, who had been the center of Marian's life. She devoured books on spirituality and began reading God's Word after many years without having done so. All along the way, the words from the note on Caitlin's laptop continued to surface in Marian's thoughts. But about four months after the Virginia Tech massacre, they became very personal to her. She heard them as though they were being spoken directly to her and she was able to believe them for herself.

Marian wrote in *Guideposts* magazine: "Caitlin's passing had brought me out of my old world and into a new one. A world where things can go wrong—more wrong than I'd ever imagined they could. But with the Lord's help, there was nothing—absolutely nothing—that could happen to me that I couldn't get through."

Today, Marian and Chris still struggle with the loss of their only child. The first Thanksgiving and Christmas after Caitlin's death was extremely difficult, and they mourn the many milestones that they'll never celebrate with Caitlin. But they also are gaining strength every day, and their relationship with God has taken on dimension and depth. Chris is seriously considering becoming a chaplain in the military, and Marian uses her own pain to give others support and love in the face of their own painful situations.

Suffering and tragedy are part of life. The Bible even tells us we will suffer and encounter trials, so we must learn how to deal with them in ways that help us overcome them instead of letting them overcome us. I like the note on Caitlin's laptop and encourage you to take it personally: "God, I know that today nothing can happen that you and I can't handle together."

We need to be balanced in our approach to growth and adversity because growth is not an automatic result of difficulty. Hardships do not necessarily produce growth or strength in us; it is not that simple. Some people shrink back or fall apart when difficulties arise. Like Marian Hammeran has learned, we grow when we determine in the midst of adversity to think and behave in godly ways. When we do what we know is right when it is difficult, uncomfortable, or inconvenient, we grow spiritually, and we are strengthened. We may have to do what is right for a long time before we feel it is "paying off," but if we stay faithful and refuse to give up, good results will come. Once we get through the adversities and challenges we face, we emerge as better people than we were when we went into them.

Determine that you will go all the way through every difficulty you might ever face in life. Make a decision now to keep going forward, no matter how difficult it is. I guarantee you'll be glad you did.

This verse has given me courage and comfort through many of my own battles in life and I believe it will also encourage you: "The Lord God is my Strength, my personal bravery, and my invincible army; He makes my feet like hinds' feet and will make me to walk [not to stand still in terror, but to walk] and make [spiritual] progress upon my high places [of trouble, suffering, or responsibility]!" (Habakkuk 3:19).

MAKE THE RIGHT CHOICES ANYWAY

An important part of never giving up is to make right choices while you are hurting, discouraged, frustrated, confused, or under pressure. The right choice is often the harder choice. And when we're in the middle of terrible stress, we naturally want to take the path of least resistance. But those are exactly the moments when you need to discipline yourself to make the tougher choice. In order to reap "right" results in life, you have to do right when you do not feel like it. I call this "pressing in and pressing on," and knowing how to do it is one of the most important components of becoming a person who never gives up.

You see, progress has a price; and becoming a person who never gives up will cost you.

> *Progress has a price; and becoming a person who never gives up will cost you.*

You will never get where you want to be in life without being willing to sacrifice and push through the obstacles and adversities that stand in your way. Your obstacle may be an attitude, a set of circumstances, a relationship, an issue from your past, a thought or mind-set, a feeling, or a bad habit. Whatever it is, you are the only one who can press through it; no one else can do your pressing for you. You may have tried to overcome your challenges in the past. Perhaps you have tried to the point that you are weary, exhausted, or discouraged. This is precisely the point where you have to summon fresh strength from God and press in one more time.

We always grow weary and may even falter in our determination if we do not continually lean on God. The Bible says that when we wait on God our strength is renewed as the eagle (see Isaiah 40:31). To wait on God means to expect Him to do what needs to be done, to lean on and rely on Him. We must make personal decisions to press through, but we never experience success in anything unless we are relying on God to help us.

One of the definitions I like for the word *press* is: "to exert steady force or pressure against something." I often say, "You have to press against the pressure that's pressing against you!" When something is pressing against you, you must be determined to press against it with greater force, because very little that is truly worthwhile or worth having in life happens without this kind of effort.

Sometimes, you have to press through natural circumstances. For example, let's say your dream is to open a business in a certain neighborhood in your city and the zoning board repeatedly rejects your request to build the facility you need. Or, maybe your dream is to go to college, but you keep getting turned down every time you apply for a scholarship.

I suffered sexual, mental, and emotional abuse as a child. Because of that, I needed to move away from home and begin supporting myself immediately after high school graduation, and I did not get to go to college. My high school teachers recognized a writing gift in me and strongly urged me to try for a college scholarship, but I was unable to do so.

However, that didn't stop God! I've written almost eighty books and never went to school to learn how to do it. I have also received several honorary degrees and two earned degrees because of my writing. I could not go to college the "normal" way, but God had another way to help me do what He wanted me to do. I am amazed when I think of what He will do if we simply refuse to give up. With Him, all things are possible!

The situations and challenges I have described in this section are real; they must be dealt with. But I am more concerned about your response to these obstacles than about the obstacles themselves, because if you can keep your thoughts and attitudes right—and if you will refuse to give up—you will eventually have the breakthrough you need. I can't promise you will get exactly what you want, but if God does not give you what you are asking for then He will give you something better. His ways are above our ways and His thoughts above our thoughts. As you think about your life and make a fresh determination to pay the price of progress, keep in mind some of the things you may need to push through:

- failure
- fear

- disappointment
- rejection
- betrayal
- jealousy
- frustration
- delay
- offense
- self-pity
- difficulties
- people's opinions
- discouragement
- weariness and fatigue
- depression
- anger
- guilt
- shame
- abuse

Of course, there are other dynamics and emotions you may also need to press through, but this list will help you recognize these things as obstacles to be overcome when you encounter them. As you face them in your life, remember, press in and press on!

GO FOR THE FRUIT

Hebrews 12:11 makes a statement I am sure most of us would agree with: "For the time being no discipline brings joy, but seems grievous and painful; but afterwards it yields a peaceable fruit of righteousness to those who have been trained by it [a harvest of fruit which consists in righteousness]."

I don't know many people who get excited about being disciplined. Disciplining ourselves is something we do because we know it is good for us and we know we need to do it, but it's not something we typically call "joyful." Although it is hard, discipline has its rewards. When we discipline ourselves to eat healthily and exercise, we gain energy and begin to be able to maintain the proper weight for our body frame. When we discipline ourselves to spend less money than we earn, we end up with a nice savings account and no pressure from debt. When we discipline ourselves to fellowship with God, pray, and study His Word, we reap the rewards of intimacy with Him.

I think about a woman who faithfully helped me in my home for several years. She used to say to me: "I wish I were small enough to wear your clothes!" She knew that I give away clothes quite frequently, but at that time my clothes were too small for her. Over and over again I heard her say, "Boy, I wish I could wear your clothes!"

Well, the day came when she finally made up her mind and said to me: "I'm going to wear your clothes. When you give away clothes, I'm going to be the first one in line because I'm right here in your house!"

This woman did not sit around wishing she was smaller, nor did she go on a crash diet. She began to change her eating habits, developed a healthier lifestyle than she had been living, and pressed through the pain of not eating foods that were wrong for her. Soon, I began to notice her getting smaller, then smaller and smaller and smaller and smaller. Over the next year, she lost fifty pounds and was able to wear my clothes. She ended up with a lot of them because she was right—it was easier to give them to her right there in my house than to load them into the car and take them somewhere else to give away.

Losing fifty pounds in twelve months required discipline, and it was not easy or joyful. But her discipline paid off and brought about the joy of a desire fulfilled in her life.

Let me call your attention to Hebrews 12:11 again: "For the time being no discipline brings joy,... but *afterwards*..." (emphasis mine). We must not buy into the lie that we should only live for the moment or that the present is all we have. We also have a future to consider, and we need to begin to live with an eye toward "afterwards," toward the "later on" times. We have to begin to care just as much or more about later on than we care about right now.

If you want to be thinner when the time comes to wear your swimsuit in June, you need to start eating healthily and exercising before summer arrives. If you want to be able to afford a new car next year, you need to work toward getting out of debt right now. If you dream of living in a nice, clean, orderly home, you have to clear out the clutter and clean it up!

Discipline may not be pleasant for your flesh while you're doing it, but it will give you a tremendous sense of satisfaction in your soul— the satisfaction that comes from knowing you are making good choices. If you will pay the price to be disciplined now, you will enjoy rewards later. If you don't pay the price to do what is right now, then you'll suffer the consequences of an undisciplined life later. You can pay now or you can pay later, but at some point, we all reap the harvest of the choices we've made. We can't simply *wish* our lives were different; we have to press through laziness, fleshly desires, and bad attitudes and refuse to give up on the discipline that will yield good fruit later on.

BE CONSISTENT

I remember a time when I had gained about ten pounds and had tried everything I could think of to lose it. My clothes were getting tight; I was very uncomfortable; and I wanted to lose the weight quickly. For a few days, I ate no fat at all. When that diet didn't work, I ate nothing but protein. When I had no success with all-protein after a couple of days, I decided to eat only nine hundred calories per day. When nothing was working and I still failed to shed my extra pounds, I tried something else and finally concluded my metabolism had gone haywire and my hormones were out of whack. As you can imagine, I became very frustrated.

One day, God spoke to me and said something very simple, but something I will never forget: *Consistency is the key*. Since that day, I have certainly found those words to be true. If we want to make progress in any area of our lives, we need to keep doing the right thing over a period of time. That is what consistency means.

Where my ten pounds were concerned, I didn't need a fad diet; I needed to eat healthily and eat reasonable amounts of food regularly, as a *lifestyle*. I knew that, but continued to struggle until the day I was reminded of a phrase in the Bible: "necessary food" (Job 23:12). God spoke to me from that scripture: *If it's not necessary, don't eat it*. That did it for me. Over the next few months, I lost those ten pounds and haven't regained them since.

The point of the stories about the lady who worked in my home and about my weight battle is to state clearly: none of us can have everything we want now and everything we want later. Remember, "For the time being no discipline brings joy…"

Let me ask you: If you're not happy with the situation you're in right now, will you make the effort to change it? Do you want to be in the same situation this time next year? Or do you want something different? If you want to have something different, then you'll have to pay the price on this end to have what you want on that end. You will have to spend some of this year moving toward your goals for next year. As you move forward, you'll have to make tough choices and you'll come to some painful crossroads. When you reach those places, you will either run back to where you came from or you will press through. If you press through, without giving up, then you'll have the victory you long for later on.

My husband is extremely healthy, and he sometimes feels better than I do physically because he has more strength and more energy. The reason for Dave's health and strength is that he has been exercising every other day since he was about sixteen years old. Like clockwork, he has made a deliberate investment in his physical well-being every other day for many years. His skin looks like that of someone thirty years younger.

I can remember looking at him wishing I didn't have any cellulite or drooping, bulging places, but wishing did not help me at all. Being jealous of Dave didn't help either. I had to start exercising myself! Now, after being diligent and consistent, I don't have nearly as many sags and bulges. I paid the price and got what I wanted!

For much of my life, I seemed to hurt myself often when I tried to exercise, so that became my excuse for not doing it. I tried to lift weights and messed up my elbow. I tried to do sit-ups and hurt my back. I now work with a strength coach who has taught me how to properly lift weights and exercise. I work out three days a week and I don't hurt myself anymore.

Dave has been paying the price to feel good for a long time. He started years ago, so he hasn't suffered the injuries I have. I'm paying the price now, and even though I'm years behind Dave, I know it's worth it. I already feel better today than I felt thirty years ago, and I expect to keep feeling better and better as I continue to exercise and take care of myself.

Another excuse that I used was that I was just too busy. I've finally realized that if we truly want to do something, we will find a way to do it. If we're too busy to be healthy then our lives are probably out of balance and we need to make some changes. Being a minister, I was busy helping people and felt I needed to sacrifice in order to do that. But I've learned that if I don't take time to take care of myself, eventually I won't be able to help anyone else either. Putting yourself at the end of the list of people you take care of is not spiritual; it is actually very foolish.

Do you need to invest in a relationship that desperately needs improvement? If you simply wait for the other person to change, the change might not ever take place. You may have to be the one to take the first step toward reconciliation. I recall a time when I felt my marital relationship was not meeting my needs. I thought of all the things I felt Dave should be doing to make me happier, but nothing changed. I even prayed about it and nothing changed. Then one day the Lord spoke to my heart, telling me I would see change if I would begin to compliment Dave often. That was difficult at first because I thought he should be doing things for me, but as I obeyed God, I saw amazing changes. It wasn't long before Dave was doing most of the things I had wanted him to do. I had to act first and then I saw results.

No matter what you want to see change, you will either press past your pain now and do what is right or you will be exactly where you are today thirty years from now—or perhaps somewhere even worse. God is a good God; He has awesome plans for your life, but you must pay the price of obedience to His Word. I encourage you to start paying today, and to keep your eye on the long-term benefits you will reap tomorrow.

DON'T YOU DARE SETTLE

I want to share with you a verse we often overlook when we read the Bible. It's Genesis 11:31: "And Terah took Abram his son, Lot the son of Haran, his grandson, and Sarai his daughter-in-law, his son Abram's wife, and they went forth together to go from Ur of the Chaldees into the land of Canaan; *but when they came to Haran, they settled there*" (emphasis mine). You may know about Abram and Sarai and Lot, but you may not have ever heard much about this man named Terah.

I believe Terah, Abram's father, failed to take an opportunity God wanted him to take. I believe God wanted Terah to go all the way to Canaan, the Promised Land, but look at the words emphasized in the scripture: "but when they came to Haran, they settled there." In other words, Terah stopped short. He was supposed to go from Ur all the way to Canaan, *but* he stopped when he reached Haran. He and his family started their journey in one place, headed for another, and before they reached their goal, their travels became so difficult they settled. They settled for much less than God had for them because they did not want to press past through pain and keep going.

I believe Abram's father could have been the one with whom God made covenant. God told him to go, but he stopped; he settled. Abram ended up receiving a phenomenal blessing, but I think God also offered it to his father. His father simply quit before he reached the place where he could receive it.

I urge you today not to settle for less than the best God has for you. Don't allow yourself to get into a position to wonder why someone else ends up with something and realize that you had the same opportunity and passed it up.

If we read on in Genesis 11, we learn that "Terah lived 205 years; and Terah died in Haran" (v. 32). He died where he settled. I think many people just settle somewhere and die in that place. They may not die physically, but their dreams die; their visions die; their passion dies; their zeal dies. Their enthusiasm for life dies. Why? Because they gave up and did not press into the best God had for them. They didn't want the pain they were facing, but they ended up with something worse—the pain of disappointment and of destiny denied.

You will face different types of pain and encounter difficulties as you go through life. You simply have to choose which kind of pain you want—the pain of pressing through or the pain of giving up. I'm convinced there is no worse pain than an unfulfilled, dissatisfied life in which you know deep down that you missed God because you didn't have the courage to press on. Don't be that way. Commit right now to go all the way with Him and to press through the challenging times.

In Genesis 12, we read the rest of the story. "Now [in Haran] the Lord said to Abram, Go for yourself [for your own advantage] away from your country, from your relatives and your father's house, to the land that I will show you" (v. 1). Here, God is asking something extremely difficult of Abram, but He also gives him the promise of a reward.

I think, in today's language, God might have said something

like this to Abram: "I know what I'm asking you to do is hard. I know you're attached to your family. I know you'll be lonely. I know packing up and walking away from everything familiar will be difficult. I know you will have lonely nights. I know people will not understand. I know they will talk about you, judge you, and criticize you. So let Me tell you what I will do for you: 'I will make of you a great nation, and I will bless you [with abundant increase of favors] and make your name famous and distinguished, and you will be a blessing [dispensing good to others]' " (v. 2). God went on to promise Abram He would bless him so much that people who came along and blessed him would be blessed, simply because they blessed him.

Throughout the Bible, we find many places where God gives a hard command, but it always comes with the promise of reward. God is not a taker; He is a giver. He never tells us to do anything unless it is for our ultimate benefit. I assure you: everything God ever asks you to do, even if it is difficult, He asks because He has something great in mind for you—but you cannot have it unless you press through that hard place. Pay the price and never give up. Victory is worth everything it costs.

I'm often humbled when I think of the extraordinary sacrifices that people have been called on to make in order to simply survive. One young man's story stands out in my mind. In February 2003, Aron Ralston, an experienced and enthusiastic outdoorsman, narrowly escaped death when caught in a fierce avalanche. In a very short time, the avalanche covered Ralston up to his neck and completely buried his skiing companion. With his considerable skill and strength, Ralston freed himself and his friend and got them both to safety.

But Ralston's alpine rescue was not his only heroic act that year. Three months later, while hiking alone through Utah's Canyonlands

> *Everything God ever asks you to do, even if it is difficult, He asks because He has something great in mind for you.*

National Park, Ralston faced another life-and-death situation, one that required him to make a desperate decision and take a drastic measure in order to stay alive.

Ralston found himself at the bottom of a hole, one hundred feet beneath the surface of the desert, miles away from a paved road, with his arm pinned to a rock wall by an eight-hundred-pound boulder. No matter how hard he tried, the boulder would not budge. Soon, the crushing pain in his hand and arm gave way to the sensation of feeling nothing at all—not a good sign.

As Ralston thought about what to do, he realized he had broken an important hiker's rule: always tell someone where you are going. No one knew where he was; no one was expecting him to return from his hiking trip for several days. By the time anyone missed him, they would not know where to search for him. By the time anyone found him, he would probably be dead. He was in such a hidden place in such a remote desert that his body might never be found.

Five days after he had been trapped, thinking death was imminent, Ralston managed to use his video camera to record messages he hoped someone would find if he did not survive. In an effort to help those who would recover his body identify him, he used his pocketknife to etch his name; the month and year of his birth, October '75; April '03, the month of his hiking trip; and "RIP," into the rock where he was stuck.

Ralston then proceeded to do the only thing he knew to do to save his life. He used his pocketknife to amputate his arm so he could be free from the boulder. Amazingly, he then applied a tourniquet and gave himself basic first aid before he managed to rappel sixty-five feet and hike seven miles out of the canyon. He was nearing the place he had parked his truck, but had to climb eight hundred feet, straight up, to reach it. Bleeding, dehydrated, and almost in shock, Ralston pushed himself to reach his vehicle. As he neared it, he saw rescue teams convening to begin searching for him.

He first received treatment at the nearest hospital, and was then transferred to another facility for surgery on the remaining portion of his arm.

I hope you will never find yourself in circumstances as drastic as Aron's, but I hope you will develop the courage, resourcefulness, and commitment to life he demonstrated when faced with a seemingly impossible situation.

Don't think or say, "This is just too hard" when you know you need to do something. God never requires us to handle more than we can bear, but with every difficulty He always provides a way for us to overcome. Never say, "There is no way," because He is the way (see John 14:6) and He makes a way for us. You can do whatever you need to do in life! You have what it takes!

The King of Denim

Have you ever put on your favorite pair of blue jeans and wondered who invented them? Maybe not, but I believe the story is worth sharing.

For years, Levi Strauss has been the most famous name in denim, but Strauss never intended to patent the popular pants or to make a fortune selling them. He was simply a smart, hardworking Bavarian immigrant determined to make a successful and prosperous life in America after he moved from what is now Germany to New York with his mother after his father died of tuberculosis in 1845. Two of Levi's older brothers, Jonas and Louis, were settled and established in their own wholesale dry goods company in New York prior to his arrival. Following in his brothers' footsteps, Levi began to learn the dry goods business.

When Levi heard about the Gold Rush in California, he decided to head west. He made his home in San Francisco, where he started a dry goods business of his own and represented his brothers' New York company as well. Through his company, he imported dry goods and sold them to small stores in California and throughout the growing towns in the western United States.

In 1872, opportunity knocked for Levi when he received a letter from a customer in Nevada. This man, a tailor named Jacob Davis, explained to Levi in his letter that he had started making pants for working men—with metal rivets in places subject to stress, such as the corners of each pocket and the base of the fly. Because he could not afford to patent the pants alone, he solicited Levi's help in paying for the necessary paperwork and suggested the two men own the patent together. On May 20, 1873, the two received their patent for what they called "waist overalls," now known as "blue jeans."

Levi soon asked Jacobs to join him in his San Francisco factory to oversee the mass production of their riveted waist overalls. At first, seamstresses sewed the pants in their homes, but by the 1880s, demand was growing, and Levi rented factory space for the production of his popular pants. The first 501® jeans, which are still available today, were produced around this time.

Over the years, Levi's business continued to grow, and he became known not only as a smart, hardworking businessman but also as a kind, friendly, down-to-earth employer. He was also a generous philanthropist who contributed large sums of money to local charities, and in 1897, he funded twenty-eight college scholarships to the University of California at Berkeley.

You must realize you will reach goals you never dreamed were possible if you continue to persevere. When you do, be kind and generous, as Levi Strauss was, and remember to share your success and rewards of your hard work with others.

CHAPTER 6

THE CONQUERER'S SPIRIT

*"Difficulties show men what they are. In case of any
difficulty remember that God has pitted you against
a rough antagonist that you may be a conqueror,
and this cannot be without toil."*

EPICTETUS

In 1867, a creative engineer named John Roebling was inspired by an idea to build a spectacular bridge connecting New York City with Brooklyn. However, bridge-building experts throughout the world thought that this was an impossible feat and told Roebling to forget the idea. It just couldn't be done. It wasn't practical. It had never been done before.

Roebling couldn't ignore the vision he had in his mind of this bridge. He thought about it all the time and knew deep in his heart that it could be done. He felt he just had to share the dream with someone else. After much discussion and persuasion he managed to convince his son Washington, an up-and-coming engineer, that the bridge in fact could be built.

Working together for the first time, the father and son developed concepts of how it could be accomplished and how the obstacles could be overcome. With great excitement and inspiration, and the headiness of a wild challenge before them, they hired their crew and began to build their dream bridge.

The project started out well, but when it was only a few months under way a tragic accident on the work site took the life of John Roebling. Three years later Washington was injured, and he suffered brain damage that left him unable to walk, talk, or even move.

"We told them so."

"Crazy men and their crazy dreams."

"It's foolish to chase wild visions."

Everyone had a negative comment to make and felt the project should be scrapped since the Roeblings were the only ones who knew how the bridge could be built. Unbelievably, in spite of his handicap, Washington was never discouraged and still had a burning desire to complete the bridge. Despite his severe handicaps, his mind was still as sharp as ever.

He tried to inspire and pass on his enthusiasm to some of his friends, but they were too daunted by the task. As he lay on his bed in his hospital room, with the sunlight streaming through the windows, a gentle breeze blew the flimsy white curtains apart and he was able to see the sky and the tops of the trees outside for just a moment.

It seemed that there was a message for him to not give up. Suddenly an idea hit him. All he could do was move one finger and he decided to make the best use of it. By moving that one finger, he slowly developed a code of communication with his wife.

He touched his wife's arm with the finger, indicating that he wanted her to call the engineers again. Then he used the same method of tapping her arm to tell the engineers what to do. It seemed foolish, but the project was under way again.

For eleven years Washington tapped out his instructions with his finger on his wife's arm until the bridge was finally completed. Today the spectacular Brooklyn Bridge stands in all its glory as a tribute to the triumph of one man's indomitable spirit and his determination not to be defeated by circumstances. It is also a tribute to the engineers and their team work, and to their faith in a man who was considered mad by half the world. It stands, too, as a tangible monument to the love and devotion of his wife, who for eleven long years patiently decoded the messages of her husband and told the engineers what to do.

—Author Unknown
  *http://www.dizzyboy.com/stories/inspirational-stories/
inspirational_story_three.html*

THE SPIRIT OF A CONQUEROR

Washington Roebling had what I call "the spirit of a conqueror," and I encourage you to get to the point where you have the spirit of a conqueror too. I want to help and inspire you to see yourself differently than you may right now, to see yourself as one who overcomes adversities, not as someone who shrinks back in fear or feels overwhelmed every time a trial comes along. I want you to be and see yourself as someone who is bold in the face of adversity and fully able to handle difficulties with courage, confidence, wisdom, and faith.

You see, adversities are not optional, and it takes a conqueror to overcome them. Jesus Himself said: "In the world you have tribulation and trials and distress and frustration; but be of good cheer [take courage; be confident, certain, undaunted]! For I have overcome the world. [I have deprived it of power to harm you and have conquered it for you]" (John 16:33).

> *Adversities are not optional, and it takes a conqueror to overcome them.*

Paul understood this, and wrote in Romans 8:35–37: "Who shall ever separate us from Christ's love? Shall suffering and affliction and tribulation? Or calamity and distress? Or persecution or hunger or destitution or peril or sword? Even as it is written, For Thy sake we are put to death all the day long; we are regarded and counted as sheep for the slaughter. Yet amid all these things we are more than conquerors and gain a surpassing victory through Him Who loved us." What does it mean to be more than a conqueror? I believe it means that before you ever face adversity, before the battle against you even begins, you already know you will win in the end if you will simply refuse to give up.

Look also at Romans 8:31: "What then shall we say to [all] this? If God is for us, who [can be] against us? [Who can be our foe, if God is on our side?]" I promise you, if God is for you, you have no reason to have any other attitude than that of a conqueror. He is on your side, and He gives you the spirit of a conqueror.

If you do not feel you have a relationship with God, you may not feel that He is for you. He is, but you need to believe that and put your faith in Him to not only forgive your sins but help you through-out your life. Please see the prayer at the end of this book. When you receive Jesus Christ into your heart, you also receive the spirit of a conqueror.

No matter what you go through in life, if you have the spirit of a conqueror and you really know who you are in Christ and truly believe God is on your side, you do not have to be daunted or overwhelmed by any difficulty you may face. Whether you are try-ing to pay off a mountain of debt, finish your education, fight an ill-ness, leave an intimidating and abusive relationship, start your own business, go into ministry, or simply clean your house, *you can do it* with God on your side. You just need to develop the spirit of a conqueror.

Remember the verse I wrote about earlier: "For the time being no discipline brings joy, but seems grievous and painful; but afterwards it yields a peaceable fruit of righteousness to those who have been trained by it" (Hebrews 12:11). When confronted with adversity, do not ever say, "I just can't take this anymore." Instead, have the spirit of a conqueror and say, "God is for me. He is on my side and I can do all things through Christ who strengthens me."

RESIST THE DEVIL

Many Christians seem to believe their faith should make them immune to the attacks and harassment of the enemy, and they act surprised when he begins to bother them. That simply is not true; as we have learned in this chapter, we *will* go through adversity. Sometimes, but not all the time, our adversities will be the work of the enemy. What we call "a run of bad luck," "a difficult situation," or "a rough day" may actually be the devil's doing. In the face of such adversities, what do we do?

First we need to remember we *do* have authority over Satan, and the Bible tells us we are to *steadfastly* resist him. James 4:7 instructs us: "So be subject to God. Resist the devil [stand firm against him], and he will flee from you." We must understand that we really do not have any power to resist Satan if we are not first submitting to God. This is so important I want to repeat it: we will not be able to exercise power over Satan if we do not first submit ourselves to God—which simply means we need to be obedient to Him. That wholehearted obedience and submission to the Lord is what gives us the authority and the ability to resist the devil.

Resisting the devil does not mean that we merely want our trials or difficulties to go away, but it means we are determined to remain steadfast and display godly behavior at all times. "He Who lives in you is greater . . . than he who is in the world" (1 John 4:4); and with God's power working in you, not only can you outlast the enemy, you can continue serving God while the battle rages.

Remember, James 4:7 says we must "stand firm" against the enemy. He will not leave simply because we respond to an altar call or wear jewelry with Christian symbols on it. He will not go away because we go to church every Sunday or have a library full of Christian books and CDs. We cannot defeat him unless we are firm in our decisions and determined to never give up.

START STRONG, FINISH WELL

Everything we undertake in life has a beginning and an end. Typically, we are excited at the beginning of an opportunity, a relationship, or a venture; we're also happy when we can celebrate our achievement and have the satisfaction of a fulfilled desire. But between the beginning and the end, every situation or pursuit has a "middle"—and the middle is where we often face our greatest challenges, hurdles, roadblocks, obstacles, detours, and tests. People who are easily led by their emotions rarely finish what they start. They give up when the project is no longer exciting and all they see in front of them is hard work. God wants us to be people who finish what we begin, and He will help us if we let Him.

You may be in the middle of a lot of things right now. Perhaps you're in the middle of getting out of debt. You have paid off all but one of your charge accounts and you're starting to think, *I've done pretty well. I think I will go shopping today because I read about a huge sale at the mall.* Doing "pretty well" is not good enough because that was not your original goal. Discipline yourself a little while longer; you will be so glad you did when you pay off that last charge account and you are completely out of debt. If you need to do something to have some fun or relieve emotional tension, find something that does not require a charge account. Whatever you find yourself in the middle of, determine to see it all the way through to the finish.

Between our beginnings and our endings we must develop the boldness and determination necessary to overcome the overwhelming circumstances we encounter in the middle. The enemy wants us to settle for less than God's best for our lives and to stop short of receiving and enjoying everything God has for us. The devil hates progress and pushes us to give up. God, on the other hand, wants the very best for us; He wants us to finish the races set before us and finish them with joy (see Hebrews 12:1). Ask yourself if you are willing to pay the price to finish.

People who finish well in life are the ones with strong character. They have "staying power." Jesus did not quit when His circumstances were rough, and He is our example. The Bible actually says we are to look away from all that distracts us unto Jesus who is the Author and Finisher of our faith (see Hebrews 12:2).

Certainly, Washington Roebling was a finisher. Another great finisher was the apostle Paul. According to Acts 20:24, none of the obstacles he faced moved him or had any sort of negative effect on him. In this verse, Paul also said he wanted to finish his course with joy. That does not mean that what he endured wasn't difficult; it simply means it did not stop him.

I think most of us want to do and be everything God intends for us, and to enjoy it along the way. Great joy comes with finishing the race God has called you to run. Enjoy the journey and keep your eyes on the prize. Jesus endured the cross for the joy of obtaining the prize that was set before Him.

Paul had a remarkable ministry and finished many things in his life. As he neared the end of his journey on earth, he wrote: "I have fought the good (worthy, honorable, and noble) fight, I have finished the race, I have kept (firmly held) the faith" (2 Timothy 4:7). In this verse, he was basically saying: "I have been through a lot. But I am still here. The enemy tried to take me out, but he did not succeed!"

I think one of the greatest testimonies we can have is summed up in these three words: "I'm still here." When we speak those words, we are saying, "I did not quit. I did not give up. I am still here."

When you feel you are in the "middle" as you reach for your goal, reread some of the stories in this book. You will be inspired by the lives of people who have done amazing things because they pressed through the middle and crossed the finish line.

DON'T BE LED ASTRAY BY DIFFICULTIES

Paul writes in 1 Thessalonians 3:3–5:

> That no one [of you] should be disturbed and beguiled and
> led astray by these afflictions and difficulties [to which
> I have referred]. For you yourselves know that this is
> [unavoidable in our position, and must be recognized as]
> our appointed lot. For even when we were with you, [you
> know] we warned you plainly beforehand that we were to be
> pressed with difficulties and made to suffer affliction, just
> as to your own knowledge it has [since] happened. That is
> the reason that, when I could bear [the suspense] no longer,
> I sent that I might learn [how you were standing the strain,
> and the endurance of] your faith, [for I was fearful] lest
> somehow the tempter had tempted you and our toil [among
> you should prove to] be fruitless and to no purpose.

In this passage, Paul was saying: "I was concerned that you would quit and give up because of all the trials and tribulations and afflictions that were coming against you." He was encouraging the Thessalonians, basically saying: "When difficulties come your way, don't be impressed by them; don't let them move you. Don't let them upset you. Just say: 'This too shall pass.' This is part of life, so don't fold under the pressure."

When Dave and I are challenged by difficulty, one of the first things he says is, "I am not impressed!" He shares that if we refuse to allow our difficulties to *impress* us, then they will not *oppress* us or *depress* us either. We must learn to hold steady in the storm and we will arrive safely at our desired destinations.

Any time we try to step out and do something for God, the enemy will oppose it. This has always been true, and it is unavoidable. Paul certainly experienced it and wrote in 1 Corinthians 16:9: "For a wide door of opportunity for effectual [service] has opened to me [there, a great and promising one], and [there are] many adversaries."

Over the years, many people have come to work at Joyce Meyer Ministries. Some of them relocate to St. Louis from other states and have to deal with the challenges of finding a place to live, moving, putting their children in school, and getting established in a new city. Some of these people have been amazed at the "many adversaries" they face during their first few weeks of employment. Over and over again, I've watched the enemy use these difficulties to make them think, *Well, maybe I didn't make the right decision after all. I thought this move was God's will, but maybe I was wrong. Maybe I should take my family and go back home where things were easier.*

Many times, Dave and I have needed to talk with these people and tell them, "The fact that you are having a difficult period of adjustment doesn't mean you didn't hear from God. You just need to hold steady. Go back to what's in your heart. Do not focus on your circumstances. Look at what's in your heart."

If they tell us that they do believe this is God's will for their lives, then Dave and I encourage them, "Then make up your mind that you're going to stay. Don't be double-minded, second-guessing your decision. Determine to push through this difficult season, and refuse to think about turning back. Since you really believe God has led you here, commit to stay—no matter what."

When we say to the enemy, "Look, devil, I know what's in my heart; I know what God told me to do; and I am going to stay here and see what God has for me, no matter how hard it is or how long it takes," then the enemy realizes he cannot control us with trials and tribulations. This builds a new level of faith and strength in us and demonstrates the spirit of a conqueror.

Paul said difficulties are unavoidable. You will face them as you continue to grow in God and follow Him. Do not let them lead you astray, but be determined to overcome them. I know you can make it. You will have to do your part, and it is going to take work, but you can do it!

DEAL WITH YOUR DIFFICULTIES

A person with the spirit of a conqueror must confront and deal with the adversities we face, not run from them. We simply cannot keep trying to escape or avoid situations that are difficult. Anytime we run from a situation, we can almost be sure we will have to go back and face it, or something very similar, at a later time in our lives.

Think about Moses. He ran from Egypt and spent forty years in the desert, where God prepared him to be a great leader. When God appeared to him in the burning bush, He basically said: "Okay, now I want you to go back to Egypt" (see Exodus 3:2–10). Yes, God sent Moses right back to the place he tried to escape.

The Bible is full of similar stories—enough to convince me that running from adversity doesn't do anyone any good. If you run from one difficult situation, there will always be another waiting for you. You see, God knows you need the skills, strength, and training you will gain from adversity, so even if you manage to get out of one difficult situation, He will lead you into another one.

For example, let's say you live next door to some people you really, really don't like. You dislike them so much that you decide to move to get away from them. Then let's say you move to a new neighborhood and your neighbors on both sides have the same personality as the people you wanted to get away from. It may be hard for you to imagine this, but it is possible that God has put them next to you. Why would He do that? Because there may be something in you that needs to be dealt with and will only surface when you are around that type of person.

I used to have an extremely difficult time with people whose personalities were similar to my father's. Because he abused me, I didn't want to be around people who spoke the way he spoke, acted the way he acted, or reminded me of him in any way.

But over a period of time I began to notice God was surrounding me with people who reminded me of my dad. Every time I encountered someone who reminded me of him, I felt insecure and fearful, and I slipped into old behavior patterns.

I didn't like my responses, nor did I understand where they came from for quite some time. But I was crying out for God to change me and show me truth. I now realize He began putting me in situations where my weaknesses would be evident so I could say: "Oh. Okay, God, I see that You want to set me free from that!" He was trying to get me to grow up and be a stronger, more mature Christian. We often ask God to deliver us from the wrong things. We want to be delivered from our trials, but we need to ask Him to deliver us from the things in our hearts that hinder His purposes for our lives.

God uses difficulties to make us people He can trust and people He can use. When we face adversity, we must have the spirit of a conqueror. David had to face Goliath before he could become king. We must not try to escape or avoid difficult situations while we are going through them. Instead, we need to say, "God, if this is something I have to go through, then I am going through it victoriously. I want to go through it with the attitude of a conqueror. Whatever You want to do in my life through this, I want You to do. But one thing I ask, God—that You help me press past my feelings and behave in a godly manner all the way through it." Getting away from trouble never needs to be our goal; our goal needs to be to conquer it with Christlike attitudes and behaviors. God teaches us to bless our enemies and pray for them (see Matthew 5:44), not to run from them. He tells us that we overcome evil with good (see Romans 12:21). No matter what is going on in your circumstances, keep doing what you know is right and you will win!

> *God uses difficulties to make us people He can trust and people He can use.*

DO IT FOR GOD

The goal I want you to have when you finish this chapter is this:
the next time you face a challenge, you will discipline your attitude,
your emotions, your mouth, and your mind to behave in a godly
manner all the way through it. That will be hard. You'll feel your
flesh rebelling against it. But keep saying, "God, I am doing this for
You. I can't do it on my own and I don't even want to do it for myself.
I want to do it for You as an act of obedience." Jesus didn't give up. He
went all the way through for us, and we can do the same for Him!

I remember one Sunday years ago when my pastor encouraged the
congregation to take a moment to say hello to other people and even
give them a hug and to tell them we loved them. I looked down the
row where I was sitting and saw a woman who had hurt me in a
significant way. I strongly sensed the Spirit of God impressing me
to give her a hug and let her know I loved her. That was going to
require great surrender for me because I felt she needed to apologize
to me and ask me to forgive her. But she had no idea she had hurt
me! Walking over to her and saying, "I love you" took everything I
had! I can't guarantee I was totally sincere, but I know I was obedient to God.

Several months later, God led me to give one of my favorite possessions to that woman. "Now God," I responded, "I don't mind giving it away. I mean, I really would like to keep it, but if You are going
to make me give it away, at least let me give to someone I like so I can
enjoy seeing her with it!"

God responded to me: *Joyce, if you can give her that, if you can
give your favorite possession to someone who really hurt you and is least
deserving of it, you will break the power of the enemy. You will destroy
his plan to destroy you.*

We do not take steps of obedience and overcome difficult times
because we feel like doing so or think obedience is a good idea. We

do it because we love God, we know He loves us, we want to obey Him, and we know His ways are always best for us.

Whatever adversities you are facing right now or will face in the days to come, I urge you to confront them, embrace them, and deal with them. Face them like a conqueror. Remember, they are working for your good and God will use them to strengthen you. Embrace them with a conqueror's attitude, and you will find yourself in a place of greater maturity, wisdom, and ability than you have ever known.

Trouble, pain, suffering, and persecution are not good in and of themselves. They come from the enemy, but God intends to work something good out of everything Satan means for harm. The situation itself may not be good, but God is good; and as we continue loving and trusting Him, He will bring good out of it (see Romans 8:28). Believing this gives us the strength and courage to keep pressing on in difficult times. We must have hope. We must believe we will see the Lord's goodness in our lives (see Psalm 27:13).

REACH YOUR FULL POTENTIAL

I fully believe reaching your potential is linked to the way you handle adversity. Winston Churchill said: "Difficulties mastered are opportunities won," and I wholeheartedly agree. If you allow difficulties and challenges to frustrate, intimidate, or discourage you, you will never overcome them. But if you face them head-on and press past the adversities you encounter, refusing to give up in the midst of them and moving forward with the spirit of a conqueror, you will develop the skills and determination needed to be everything you were created to be and experience everything God intends for you.

From Cotton Field to Corporation

The woman who came to be known as Madam C. J. Walker, the first African American female millionaire in the United States was born Sarah Breedlove on a Louisiana plantation in 1867, to former slaves who both died and left her an orphan by the time she was seven years old. She and her sister survived because they were willing to do the grueling, dirty work of picking cotton in the fields of Louisiana and Mississippi.

When she was fourteen, she married a man who died six years later, leaving her alone with a young daughter. Sarah and her daughter moved to St. Louis, Missouri, where her four brothers had found work as successful barbers, and she took a job as a washer-woman, earning $1.50 per day.

During the 1890s, Sarah found herself with a strange scalp condition that caused her to lose most of her hair. She tried every possible remedy to make her hair grow back, but nothing was effective.

Sarah took a job as a sales representative for a hair products company and moved to Denver, Colorado, where she met and married Charles Joseph Walker, and became known as "Madam C. J. Walker."

Still suffering with hair loss, Sarah finally found a solution—in an unusual way. She dreamed about an old man, who told her which ingredients to combine to make her hair grow back. The next day, she mixed the ingredients, tried the remedy, and it was successful!

Madam C. J. Walker quickly realized she had a product she could market and sell, so she opened her own business, producing and distributing "Madam Walker's Wonderful Hair Grower."

(continued)

To get her business off to a strong start, Madam Walker logged many miles as she personally traveled the United States for more than a year, going door-to-door telling people about her products and giving presentations wherever she could find an audience. With diligence and determination, she continued to develop and perfect strategies for increasingly effective sales and marketing of her products.

In 1908, Madam Walker went to Pittsburgh, Pennsylvania, to open a school to train a team of "Walker hair culturists" to help her in her growing business. Two years later, she had made her home and built a factory for the production and distribution of her products in Indianapolis—the metropolis of manufacturing in her day. Before the end of her first year in Indianapolis, Madam Walker gave one thousand dollars toward the building of a local YMCA for African Americans—a remarkable achievement for a woman who once supported herself by picking cotton, but one made possible because she worked hard and refused to give up.

In 1916, Madam Walker left Indianapolis for New York, though her Indianapolis factory continued to operate under the leadership of the forewoman she had trained. Because she refused to give up in the face of the personal problem of hair loss, Madam C. J. Walker went from picking cotton to being a pioneer in the beauty industry and the first African American woman to become a millionaire in the United States. Let her story inspire you to not give up when you face challenges, but to be creative, work hard, and persevere until you reach your full potential.

CHAPTER 7

NEVER GIVE UP ON WHAT'S IMPORTANT TO YOU

"The fishermen know that the sea is dangerous and the storm terrible, but they have never found these dangers sufficient reason for remaining ashore."
VINCENT VAN GOGH

What's important to you? When you stop and think about it, what really matters to you? Is it your job, your reputation, your health, your family, your relationship with God, your possessions, a project, or a cause?

Different things are important to different people. In Old Testament times, rebuilding the devastated walls of his hometown of Jerusalem was extremely important to a man named Nehemiah. It was so important he asked his employer, the king of Persia, to allow him to return to Jerusalem to oversee this project, and the king granted it.

Nehemiah definitely had the spirit of a conqueror, as you'll see as you read his story. He faced a storm of opposition, ridicule, and intimidation as he tried to finish the task so important to him, the project God called him to complete. Similarly, you will face various kinds of storms as you endeavor to do what is important to you.

Nehemiah's story will teach you how to weather them well and emerge victorious.

TAKE COVER

The best way to be safe through a natural storm is to take cover. If you do not seek shelter, the wind will blow you this way and that, and the rain may keep you from being able to see clearly. Besides that, you might get struck by lightning. If you do not take cover, the storm is in control of you. But if you will position yourself indoors through the storm, you will be able to ride it out and be in good shape to do what you need to do when it passes.

Psalm 91:1 gives us instructions for the spiritual storms of life: "He who dwells in the secret place of the Most High shall remain stable and fixed under the shadow the Almighty [Whose power no foe can withstand]." The first place you need to run when a storm hits in your life is to the secret place of the Most High, the presence of God. Read His Word; pray; worship Him; tell Him you trust Him as the winds of adversity blow. These are the spiritual disciplines no foe can withstand. When you practice these habits, you actually construct spiritual walls of protection around yourself. They will not keep the storms of life away, but they will provide protection and enable you to stand strong against them.

Many of life's storms come directly from the enemy. He is a master at orchestrating circumstances that will devastate a life, a dream, a marriage, a family, a business, a school, or a geographic region. He does not want you to build walls of protection around your life. He wants all your walls torn down so he can keep attacking you successfully.

WALLS KEEP THE ENEMY OUT

Upon his arrival in Jerusalem, Nehemiah saw the enemies of God's people were taking advantage of them because the city had no walls to keep the enemies out. When he first met with the people of Jerusalem, he said: "You see the bad situation we are in—how Jerusalem lies in ruins, and its gates are burned with fire. Come, let us build up the wall of Jerusalem, that we may no longer be a disgrace. Then I told them of the hand of my God which was upon me for good, and also the words that the king had spoken to me. And they said, Let us rise up and build! So they strengthened their hands for the good work" (Nehemiah 2:17–18).

The same principles in this story apply to you when you realize your life is a mess and the enemy is attacking you because of the way you have lived. You haven't kept your walls up; you have no protection. But with God's help you can begin now to build the right kind of life; you can start building walls of protection around yourself so you are protected from the enemy. He may come against you, but his plans will not succeed.

If you feel the storms of life have left you battered and tattered for too long and are ready to build some walls of protection, I'm excited for you. But don't expect to do it without opposition. That's just a reality of life. Any time you begin to move forward and do what is right, the enemy will be unhappy. But you don't need to worry about the opposition, because you have what it takes to win every battle. God is for you, in you, with you, and around you. He also works through you to not only win your own battles but to help other people win theirs.

A STORM IS BREWIN'

No sooner had the Jews "strengthened their hands for the good work," than opposition arose. When people began to hear of the rebuilding effort, they ridiculed Nehemiah and the Jews. Three men particularly—Sanballat, Tobiah, and Geshem—began to mock and make fun of them. "They laughed us to scorn and despised us and said, What is this thing you are doing?" (Nehemiah 2:19).

I can remember a similar experience. I wrote earlier about how people responded to me when I received God's call on my life. Many people laughed at me and said, "What do you think you are doing?" This was an extremely difficult time for me, but I did my best to stand through the storm of disapproval. I did everything I could to stay as close to God as possible through studying His Word, praying, and spending time in His presence. I worked to improve my attitudes and my marriage and my relationships with my children. Even in the midst of being misunderstood and laughed at, I kept working with God to overcome my problems and build a healthy self-image through learning about His love and mercy. By doing this, I was building walls of protection. I was putting bricks in my wall as diligently as I could, but the enemy continued to fight against me.

Have you ever been trying as hard as you could to do what was right but felt that the storm raged even stronger? I remember a specific situation that was especially difficult for me. One day, someone I considered a friend walked up to me and said: "Joyce, someone told me you believe God is going to give you one of the largest ministries run by a woman in the whole country. Did you say that?"

I responded, "Yes, I really believe God spoke that to me."

This woman snickered and said, "Well, to tell you the truth, some of us have been talking about that, and we just think that is impossible with your personality."

Hearing such comments is like being in the middle of a violent storm with no protection. I felt as Nehemiah must have felt when Sanballat, Tobiah, and Geshem said to him, between bursts of laughter: "What on earth do you think you are doing? You can't do that!"

Nehemiah stood firm and demonstrated the spirit of a conqueror when he said, "The God of heaven will prosper us; therefore we His servants will arise and build, but you have no portion or right or memorial in Jerusalem" (Nehemiah 2:20).

When the enemy comes against you, you also have to say, "You have no right here. You can have no portion of me, nor can you hinder God's will for my life!" If you have given your life to Jesus Christ, you belong to Him, not to the devil. You simply have to remind him of that fact and resist him. You do not have to raise your voice or be dramatic, but you do need to use your authority in Christ and say: "No way, devil. You are not going to stop me. I will not give up on this. No matter what you throw at me, I will not quit!'

I refused to quit and eventually the woman who told me she and her friends thought it was impossible for me to succeed ended up working for me. God always vindicates us if we just keep doing what He tells us to do. Don't ever give up just because someone tells you that you can't succeed.

> *Don't ever give up just because someone tells you that you can't succeed.*

To stand against the enemy in the storms of life, we really must be determined. Sometimes we simply give up too easily. We get a little bit discouraged, or the "Sanballats" of life hurt our feelings, and we begin to cave under the pressure. Never forget that, according to God's Word, *you are more than a conqueror* (see Romans 8:37).

NOT EVERYONE LIKES PROGRESS

Sanballat was a formidable enemy; he did not give up easily. When he heard the building of the city walls was going forward in spite of his objections, "he was angry and in a great rage, and he ridiculed the Jews" (Nehemiah 4:1). The more they built, the angrier he became.

Maybe you know people who become angry when others try to make progress, better themselves, or do something new and different. Why would people become angry about your progress? Because people who do not want to progress themselves do not want you to progress either. They would rather judge you critically than face the fact that they do not really want to make the effort necessary to improve their lives or follow their dreams. Instead of investing in their futures and pursuing their destinies, they prefer to become angry and act as though something is wrong with you. That way, they do not have to consider the possibility that something may be wrong with them. It is called "blame shifting," and people who do it do not want to be blamed for not making right choices so they shift the focus to you and try to discredit you.

Sanballat and his buddies flew into "a great rage" because Nehemiah was leading an effort to help people and improve the community. In your efforts to help yourself and the people around you, do not be surprised if you meet with someone who becomes angry and critical about it. Just stand through that storm; hold your peace; and keep doing what you believe in your heart to be right.

WHAT A MESS!

Sanballat continued his angry rant in Nehemiah 4:2: "And he said before his brethren and the army of Samaria, What are these feeble Jews doing? Will they restore things [at will and by themselves]? Will they [try to bribe their God] with sacrifices? Will they finish up in a day? Will they revive the stones out of the heaps of rubbish, seeing that they are burned?"

Basically, Sanballat was saying, "This mess is too big to ever rebuild!" Yes, the walls were so destroyed that they were nothing more than heaps of charred stones. They were not good building materials for walls—at least not without a lot of effort. In Sanballat's mind, building the walls was a bad idea. They were simply too far gone.

The enemy may be hurling the same accusations at you: "What do you mean you can start over? Look at what a mess your life is in!" "There is no way you can get a college degree, not with the way your mind has been messed up!" "You think you're going to save enough money to send your children to college? Your finances are in such a mess the bank can't even straighten them out!" Whatever he is saying to you, I want you to know you are never too big a mess for God to redeem and nothing is beyond His ability to restore.

If anyone's life has ever been a mess, mine was. If anyone had reason to believe trying to get better simply wasn't worth the effort, I did. And the enemy knew it too. He tried to convince me many times that I would never have a normal life. He told me I would never be "quite right," that I would never be able to have a healthy self-image because I was an incest victim. He said I wouldn't be able to trust men because of the way men had treated me, that I could never have a relationship of godly submission to my husband; that I could never stop trying to control everything around me or keep from losing my temper because of the repressed anger in me. He told me I could never be sweet and nice and kind, and that I would always be rough, harsh, hard, rude, and crude because of the way I was raised. I desperately wanted to change and be the kind of woman I believe God wanted me to be, but I had to stand strong through the battle raging in my mind and emotions.

The devil is a liar; it's that simple (see John 8:44). He does not tell you the truth; he tells you whatever he wants to tell you in order to destroy you. He relentlessly attacks your mind and emotions. When you are tempted to give up because you think your problems are too big, just remember, the devil is a liar and nothing is impossible with God!

The devil hates all progress. Even if you commit to lose a certain amount of weight and do well on your diet for a week, then lose your willpower one day and eat a hot fudge sundae, the enemy will be right there to say: "See? This is too hard. You cannot do it. You have always been overweight and your eating habits are too ingrained in you for you to try to change them now!"

When he sends a storm of accusations against you, stand up and say: "Listen, *liar!* I had a little setback, but it is not over yet! I will meet my goals. I will do what God is calling me to do. It *is* worth the effort, and you will not stop me!" Fight the good fight of faith. You are a soldier in the army of the God, and He is on your side.

We may all have setbacks when we are learning how to do things correctly, but we can have a fresh start every day. All babies fall down while trying to learn how to walk. When they take a tumble, they do not just lie on the floor and cry for the rest of their lives. They get up, dust themselves off, and try again! No matter how many times they fall, they never give up.

PRAY!

In Nehemiah 4:4, we find three words that are vitally important to remember when we are trying to stand through a storm: "And Nehemiah prayed." How did he respond to all the attacks that came against him—the laughing, the anger, the rage, the judgment, the criticism, being told his desired goal was impossible? He prayed!

Let me ask you: What would happen if you prayed every single time you felt afraid or intimidated? What if you prayed every time you were offended, or every time someone hurt your feelings? What if you prayed immediately every time some kind of judgment or criticism came against you? Would your life be different? Would you be able to withstand those storms better? Of course you would.

We can learn an important lesson from Nehemiah's prayer: "Hear, O our God," he said, "for we are despised. Turn their taunts upon their own heads, and give them for a prey in a land of their captivity" (Nehemiah 4:4). Notice that Nehemiah didn't go after his enemies himself; he asked *God* to deal with them. His attitude was, "I'm doing Your will! You told me to build this wall and I am busy building it. You will have to take care of my enemies!"

Many times God tells us to do something or gives us an assignment and we begin doing it. But then the enemy comes against us, and when we turn to fight him, we turn away from God. Suddenly, the enemy has all of our attention. We spend our time fighting him instead of praying and asking God to intervene.

Nehemiah knew better than to let his enemies command his focus. He was aware of them, but he kept his eyes on God and the job God called him to do. And he simply prayed and asked God to deal with those who were attacking him.

Most of us will never forget September 11, 2001. I recently read an inspiring story about Stanley Praimnath, a banker who worked in Tower Two of the World Trade Center and miraculously survived the attacks. Stanley recalls: "For some particular reason, I gave the Lord a little extra of myself that morning [during prayer]. I said, 'Lord, cover me and all my loved ones under your precious blood.' And even though I said that and believed it, I said it over and over and over."

Soon after he arrived at his office on the eighty-first floor, Stanley glanced out of his window and saw Tower One on fire. He and a co-worker decided to evacuate their building, but returned to his office after a security guard assured them Tower Two was safe and secure.

Stanley reached his office just in time to catch a phone call from someone who asked him if he was watching the news. He responded that everything was fine. Then he looked up and saw an American Airlines jet heading straight for him. All he could think to do was dive under his desk, curl into a fetal position, and pray as the plane crashed about twenty feet from him and exploded. Once he got there, he said, he knew "beyond a shadow of a doubt that the Lord was going to take care of [him]."

Stanley saw a wing of the plane ablaze in the doorway to the offices of his department. Miraculously unhurt, he knew he needed to get out of the building, but he was trapped in rubble and could not move.

Stanley prayed fervently, asking God to spare his life and saying, "Lord, you take control. This is your problem now." He remembers suddenly feeling like "the strongest man alive" as strength surged through his body and enabled him to shake off the debris that held him captive. He climbed over the destruction around him and dodged flickering flames saying, "Lord, I have to go home to my loved ones. I have to make it. You have to help me."

Cut and bruised, Stanley stumbled through the dangerous remains of his office, only to realize all exits were blocked. He was trapped against a wall. He fell to his knees and began to pray again, then asked someone on the other side of the wall, "Do you know Jesus?" When the man said yes, the two of them prayed and asked God to help them break through the wall. They did, and Stanley climbed through a small hole, now able to reach the staircase of the collapsing building.

He and his new friend started down the stairs, stopping at every floor to see if anyone needed help. By the time they reached the concourse, the only people they saw were firefighters yelling, "Run! Run!"

The men wanted to run, but were surrounded by fire. If they didn't run through the flames, they would be burned to death. They doused themselves in water under the building's sprinkler system and darted through the flames to safety at last.

Stanley was determined to survive a life-threatening situation, but he could not do it without God's help. While human determination is vital to never giving up, we need to remember to rely on God in every situation, never trying to "make things happen" in our own strength, but doing our part to persevere, while counting on God to bring the breakthrough we need.

I want you to know this: the enemy is really not your problem; he is God's problem. You will waste your time if you turn your attention away from your God-given assignments and opportunities and begin to focus on the enemy. Satan knows that if he can distract you, he can ultimately defeat you. God is your defender; He promises to fight your battles for you. So when the enemy begins to stir up a storm in your life, be like Nehemiah: pray.

A HEART AND MIND TO WORK

Nehemiah has a good report in chapter 4: "So we built the wall, and all [of it] was joined together to half its height, for the people had a heart and mind to work" (v. 6). Clearly, Nehemiah's people were determined to work, even though their enemies came against them persistently. Even though their enemies were stubborn, they would not keep from building!

The enemy cannot hold you back if you are determined! You will have to be more determined than he is, but you can do it because God is on your side. The enemy may oppose you fiercely, but you can build your walls of protection and achieve your goals in life if you simply refuse to give up.

Not only did the walls begin to go up, but the breaches in the walls were being closed, the cracks were being sealed. This made Nehemiah's enemies really furious.

I believe one of the benefits of your reading this book is that the "cracks" in your life will be closed! Any places that may be weak in you are being strengthened as you learn how to be a person who never gives up. This makes the enemy angry, very angry, because he does not want you to move forward in God's purposes for your life.

Some people become afraid when they think the enemy is angry, but there's no need to fear. God is on your side, and He always leads you in triumph (see 2 Corinthians 2:14). To defeat an angry enemy, seek God, stay in His Word, worship Him, and pray, as Nehemiah did. Do not allow yourself to think you have to try to defeat the devil on your own! Pray—keep on doing what you know God is telling you to do! Pray— and keep on doing what you know the devil does not want you to do!

Nehemiah never stopped praying. I wrote about his prayer earlier, but we see him praying again in Nehemiah 4:9: "But because of them we made our prayer to our God and set a watch against them day and night." In other words, they prayed consistently.

I encourage you to pray at all times, not just when you face a crisis. You do not need God only in the midst of disasters; you need Him all the time. Cultivate a lifestyle of prayer, because that is one way you build a wall of protection around yourself and those you love. To learn more about prayer, I suggest my book *The Power of Simple Prayer*.

FIGHT, DON'T FEAR

You can tell by now Nehemiah was a strong and wise leader. Not only did he seek and rely on God, he also made smart decisions and knew how to keep the people encouraged. Nehemiah 4:13–14 says:

> So I set armed men behind the wall in places where it was least protected; and I even thus used the people as families with their swords, spears, and bows. I looked [them over] and rose up and said to the nobles and officials and the other people, Do not be afraid of the enemy; [earnestly] remember the Lord and imprint Him [on your minds], great and terrible, and [take from Him courage to] fight for your brethren, your sons, your daughters, your wives, and your homes (emphasis mine).

I want to echo Nehemiah's words to you today: Fight for your home! Fight for your children! Fight for your right to live free from guilt and condemnation! Fight for your right to live under the grace of God and not be bound to legalism. Fight for your right to be happy! Fight for the dreams God has put in your heart! Fight for what is important to you! Refuse to settle for anything less than everything God has for you. The enemy will come against you, but do not be afraid of him. Instead, remember the Lord and take your courage from Him.

> *Refuse to settle for anything less than everything God has for you.*

After this point in Nehemiah's story, he had a measure of victory: "And when our enemies heard that their plot was known to us and that God had frustrated their purposes, we all returned to the wall, everyone to his work. And from that time forth, half of my servants worked at the task, and the other half held the spears, shields, bows, and coats of mail; and the leaders stood behind all the house of Judah" (vv. 15–16).

The important lesson we learn here is that we must not let down our guard when we experience some relief or a level of victory. We want to be completely free, not merely to get a little relief. Nehemiah could have said, "Listen, everybody! Our enemies know we found out what they were plotting against us. They know God has frustrated their purposes! We can all relax!" But instead, Nehemiah wisely maintained an army against the enemy, even though he knew the enemy had retreated somewhat. He kept the same attitude he had all along: "We are contending to do what God wants us to do. Therefore, we can't slack off; we can't let up; we have to continue to think like fighters, even though our enemy is not active against us at the moment."

TAKE YOUR WEAPON TO WORK

Nehemiah knew how to get a job done. We can read about his strategy in Nehemiah 4:17–18: "Those who built the wall and those who bore burdens loaded themselves so that everyone worked with one hand and held a weapon with the other hand, and every builder had his sword girded by his side, and so worked. And he who sounded the trumpet was at my side."

One of the ways we work with one hand and hold a weapon in the other is to praise God while we work. No matter what you're trying to build—your home, your marriage, your business, financial security, an exercise plan, or an intimate relationship with God—do not forget to worship as you work. Remember to praise God and thank Him for even small steps of progress. You don't have to make a production out of your praise; just keep a thankful heart and an attitude that says, "I love You, Lord. I worship You. I can't do this without You. I need Your help today. Thank You for giving me a goal to work toward and for helping me to accomplish it."

I believe the sword that Nehemiah's builders kept by their sides represents our need to keep God's Word with us all the time. God's Word is a sword for us, and we have to wield it against the enemy. Our swords will not do any good if we keep them in their sheaths, just as a Bible won't help us if it just sits on a shelf gathering dust. They will not be effective against the enemy if we do not use them. To use our swords is to know, believe, and speak the Word of God.

If you wake up one morning and feel you want to give up, use your sword by saying: "I will not give up! God has plans to give me a future and a hope and I am going to keep working so I can experience them!" (see Jeremiah 29:11). God gives us weapons of warfare so we can use them. If you want to win, you will have to remain active. Passivity and wishing never win the battle.

THE REST OF THE STORY

I know you want to know what happened to Nehemiah and the wall. You can read the entire story in the book of Nehemiah, but let me say the project was a success. Nehemiah and the people had to fight their enemies until the walls were finished. He had to stand up to government officials who were not treating the people fairly, and Sanballat continued to pester him and even made one last effort to stop him through intimidation.

When the wall was finished, how do you think the enemies of God's people responded? "When all our enemies heard of it, all the nations around us feared and fell far in their own esteem, for they saw that this work was done by our God" (Nehemiah 6:16).

Even after the building of the wall was complete, Tobiah continued to send threatening letters to Nehemiah. The enemy did not go away, but he didn't stop Nehemiah from completing his task either. Nehemiah learned to stand through the storms of the enemies' assaults, to contend for what was important to him, and to emerge victorious. That is exactly what God wants for you.

The Integrity of a Penney

A poor minister's son from Missouri, James Cash Penney founded one of America's most successful retail businesses on the simple, timeless values of honesty, integrity, respect, and hard work.

In addition to his work as a minister, Penney's father was a farmer, and Penney learned to work on the family farm near Hamilton, Missouri. His father wanted to make sure his children understood the value of money, so he made James work to buy his own clothes, starting at eight years old.

In 1893, Penney graduated from high school, hoping to become a lawyer. Instead, he became a salesman at a local dry goods store, J. M. Hale and Brothers. Penney soon learned that everyone did not live by the same values he held dear. Other clerks took business away from him and he had to learn to be more confident, strengthen his sales skills, and stand up for the sales opportunities that were rightfully his.

In the midst of this time of personal and professional growth, Penney's health began to decline. In danger of contracting tuberculosis, his doctor urged him to relocate from Missouri to a drier climate. He ended up in Denver, Colorado, where he found employment in the dry goods trade he had learned from Mr. Hale.

The industrious and ambitious Penney soon had enough money saved to start his own business, so he opened a butcher shop. It failed, but not because Penney was a bad businessman; it failed because of his integrity. Penney believed in treating all customers with kindness and respect, and when he refused to grant special treatment to a certain influential customer, that customer used his influence to force Penney out of business.

Following the closing of the butcher shop, Penney went to

(continued)

work for the chain of Golden Rule dry goods stores. He enjoyed success there, and eventually became a partner in the company. While working for Golden Rule and living in Wyoming, Penney fell in love with Berta Alva Hess, and married her.

Based on his philosophy of honesty, integrity, and respect, Penney's business continued to grow and he soon opened his own Golden Rule store. He provided quality merchandise at reasonable prices for working-class families and developed a reputation for excellent service. He refused to take credit, requiring customers to pay cash for their purchases.

The owners of Golden Rule eventually sold out to Penney and he changed the chain's name to J. C. Penney Company. Penney moved the company's headquarters to New York in 1914 and opened the first official J. C. Penney store in Missouri in 1918.

Penney had several personal tragedies to overcome as he continued to build his retail empire. In 1910, he suffered the devastating loss of his wife, Berta, who succumbed to pneumonia, leaving him to raise two sons alone. He wrote that her death caused his world to "crash" around him. In 1919, Penney married again. His wife, Mary, bore him a son, but died in 1923, leaving him a widower again. In 1926, he married again. He and his wife, Caroline, had two daughters and remained married until Penney's death.

J. C. Penney built a thriving business and a life upon good, godly principles. He never gave up on his integrity. No matter what you try to accomplish in life, hold fast to the principles in God's Word and you will *always* be successful.

CHAPTER 8

THE KEYS TO SUCCESS

"Our greatest weakness lies in giving up. The most certain way to succeed is always to try just one more time."
THOMAS EDISON

There are four keys to success in any endeavor you undertake: commitment, determination, waiting on the Lord, and taking time to be refreshed and renewed. If these character traits and habits will become part of the routine of your life, they'll keep you from giving up and move you toward the success you long for.

COMMITMENT

If you want to summarize in one word the idea of "never give up", you can use the word *commitment*. Without commitment, people give up easily; they have no staying power at all. If you want to be one who never gives up, commitment is the key.

Radically Committed

When an eaglet is about one year old, he begins to develop some independence. His eyesight is good at this point, and his talons are sharp. He can find his own food, fly, and even soar a little bit. He lives his life as a young eagle for about three more years, continuing to grow and gain strength, improving in all his abilities, and just getting established in life as an eagle.

But by the time the eagle is about four years old, he begins to change—not deliberately, but instinctively. He feels uncomfortable inside, strange, and uneasy. He probably does not understand what is happening to him. Eventually, in the midst of this strange season of growth, he begins to realize he was not created only to live for his own pleasure. He wants his life to be about more than himself.

At that point, the male eagle leaves to find a female. When he finds one, they begin a game of tag, which is actually a type of courtship. His uneasiness is a longing for love! It is time for him to grow up. The female eagle soars high in the sky in a figure-eight pattern and makes the male eagle chase her. Now he is no longer flying his own course; he is following someone else—someone who appears to be going in a strange direction.

After a little while she dives to the ground, picks up a twig, flies up to about ten thousand feet, and drops the twig. He dives at approximately two hundred miles per hour to catch the twig in midair and takes it back to her. What is her response? She ignores him.

At this point, even though he probably feels very insulted, he has a decision to make: "Am I going to really get committed and see this through to the finish? Is this really what I want? Or should I just forget about this and find something a little easier to do with my time?"

The female eagle repeats this process, and she makes the male's job increasingly difficult. Each time she flies, the twig gets larger and she flies at a lower altitude. That means the twig is going to hit the ground faster, and the male will have to work harder if he wants to win her over.

This game can literally go on for days. Finally, the female gets a branch that is heavier than the male eagle. I can imagine he would want to say, "This is not fair! Now, God, You *know* I can't do that!

Come on, God, You *know* that is too much for me!" This time the female flies only five hundred feet above the ground and drops the branch. If he catches it, they go on together. If not, she flies off and leaves him; she has decided to wait for a male eagle who has the tenacity to be her man.

For the male eagle to continue this process, he must be extremely committed. Once he passes the final twig test, both eagles move from courtship to the final commitment test. She flies high into the sky; he chases her; and suddenly she makes an odd move. In midair, she flips over on her back and sticks her talons up. The male moves over her and locks his talons with hers while they fall toward the earth. At this point he has made up his mind. He is committed, and he would die rather than let her go. Now they begin to sing a love song. They mate for life. Neither of them ever has another mate unless one of them dies. If the female dies, the male raises the young.

Even after the mating process is finished and she is his and they are in their nest, the male eagle continues to court the female for the rest of their lives. Male eagles have been seen to stroke the feathers of their female companions and to bring green twigs home to them long after the courtship is complete. If you are a woman reading this, you are probably wishing every man on earth would learn a few things from the eagle!

This is the kind of commitment that stays steady and strong throughout the course of a lifetime, and I hope it is the kind of commitment you will develop in your life. You may not have it down perfectly, but if you want to move on with God and be blessed in your life, you need this kind of radical commitment—the kind that follows through even when times are tough, when you feel alone or rejected, or when circumstances look bad. Think of the mighty male eagle who stays committed, even though his commitment could cost him his life. And learn to say from the core of your being, "Nothing is going to shake my commitment in this situation. I am going to see it through to the finish. *I will not give up,* no matter what."

God, the Eagle, and You

Many times we find ourselves feeling uncomfortable for the same reason the four-year-old eagle does: it's time for us to grow up. We often feel a vague sort of discontentment and struggle with a sense of restlessness when God wants to take us to a new level. The way to respond is to keep our thoughts clear and our emotions calm because chances are, nothing is seriously wrong at all. The time has simply come to grow stronger and become more mature, and we need to commit to the process.

Is commitment easy? No, but it is worth all it requires. I have fought many battles in life, but I'm now very happy, fulfilled, and satisfied. No, it hasn't been easy, and yes, I've wanted to give up many, many times. But I am committed to God and to the work of ministry to which He has called me. That doesn't mean I'm never tempted to give up; it just means that the strength of my commitment enables me to resist that temptation.

> Is commitment easy? No, but it is worth all it requires.

God wants to take you to a new level of commitment. He wants you, like the eagle, to be fiercely committed to His purposes for your life and to dedicate yourself to Him. He wants you to be in a committed relationship with Him—for life. I can't imagine anything more satisfying, more rewarding, or more adventuresome. He has more in store for you than you have ever asked or imagined, but in order to see His plans become a reality in your life you will need to be very committed!

DETERMINATION

When we receive Christ as our Savior we receive God's Spirit; we receive a new "want-to," a determination that enables us to achieve goals and pursue dreams that seem impossible. In fact, your want-to is one of the strongest forces on earth. If it is turned in the right direction, you will be able to accomplish amazing things in life. I have discovered in my own life that I should not make excuses for anything because the truth is simply this: if I really want to do something, I will do it!

Born in inner-city Detroit to a woman who dropped out of school in the third grade and married when she was only thirteen, renowned pediatric neurosurgeon Ben Carson had a rough start. His parents divorced when he was eight years old, and as a result, his mother worked two or three jobs at a time simply to provide Ben and his brother, Curtis, with the basic needs of life. His "never give up" story is as much a testimony to her determination and perseverance as it is to his.

Neither Ben nor Curtis performed well in school. By the time Ben was in fifth grade, he had the worst grades in his class and other students referred to him as "dummy." During this time, he demonstrated uncontrollable anger and a volatile temper.

Ben's problems concerned his mother greatly. She knew she had to do something. First, she began to pray, and she prayed fervently that she would have the wisdom to know what to do to help Ben and Curtis learn the lessons they needed to know and do well in school. She then instituted strict discipline at home, limiting the time the boys could spend watching television, prohibiting them from playing until they finished their homework assignments each day, and requiring them to read and write reports on two books per week. As a result of the focused attention Ben gave to his schoolwork and his voracious reading habits, Ben not only improved his grades dramatically but also became convinced he was not "dumb" and could learn as well as anyone else. Over time, he learned to control his temper and get along well with others.

By the time he finished high school, Ben was an outstanding student. He graduated with honors and went on to Yale University, where he received a degree in psychology and had plans to continue his education by preparing to be a psychiatrist. Once in medical school, at the University of Michigan, Ben decided to pursue neuro-surgery instead of psychiatry. Ben completed his residency in neu-rosurgery at one of the most respected hospitals in the world, Johns Hopkins in Baltimore, Maryland, and by the time he was in his early thirties, he was that hospital's director of pediatric neurosurgery—the youngest person to ever hold such a position at Johns Hopkins. As of this writing, he remains in this position; serves as a profes-sor of neurological surgery, oncology, plastic surgery, and pediatrics at Johns Hopkins medical school; and maintains a busy schedule speaking to and encouraging young people to maximize their intel-lectual potential.

If you dream of reaching a goal that seems impossible, remember Ben Carson, who went from being the lowest achiever in his class to being one of the brightest medical minds in the world today. It was possible for him because his mother refused to give up on him and he never gave up on himself.

If you are the parent of a child who struggles in school or in any area of life, let the story of Ben Carson inspire you. Remember what a difference his mother made in his life, and do as she did: pray and ask God to give you wisdom to help your children succeed. Then help them apply the discipline they need and don't let them give up!

If you really want to come out of the bondage that's holding you captive, you will! If you really want to break free from your past and move beyond it, you will. If you really want to develop a posi-tive attitude instead of having a negative one, you will. If you really want to wait and marry the right person and not take "second best" because you fear no one else will come along, you will!

If you're determined enough, nobody—no evil force from hell, no person on earth—can stop you from being successful. If you will obey God and do what He tells you to do, and if you will be deter-mined to outlast the devil every single time he comes against you, then nothing will be able to keep you from reaching your goals.

Be Determined

One of the definitions of *determine* is: "to settle a dispute by an authoritative decision or a pronouncement." This definition encourages me, because I make "pronouncements" often as a way of building my determination in certain areas. Sometimes, when I know I have eaten enough, but my flesh still wants to eat more, I sit at the table and announce aloud: "This is my last bite! I am *finished* with this meal!"

When you are determined in a particular area, you may have to talk to yourself in a similar way. Sometimes the best way to overcome the temptation to give up on something is to say to yourself, "Oh no, you don't! Stop your whining and straighten up right this minute!" Over the years, when I have felt like giving up and had no one to encourage me, I have said to myself: "Joyce, you can make it! It may be hard, but you *can* make it and don't you dare think you can't!"

At one point in my life, I went through a ten-year period of suffering from various physical problems. *Ten years!* I had

> *Sometimes the best way to overcome the temptation to give up on something is to say to yourself, "Oh no, you don't! Stop your whining and straighten up right this minute!"*

lots of symptoms, some of which involved low blood sugar, but most of which were rooted in stress caused from working too hard. I was also going through the "change of life," which was not easy for me. Hormone changes in my body caused migraine headaches and at one point in 1989, as I mentioned, I even had breast cancer and needed surgery.

I can't count the number of times during those ten years I walked onto a platform to preach thinking, *I wonder if I can stand here long enough to preach my message.* I prayed fervently for God to heal me. He did not take away my problems completely, but He did give me strength to do what I needed to do *in spite of them*—every single time. But I didn't want the strength to press through; I wanted the problems gone! Trying to keep going through those years was hard, *really* hard, but I was determined to not be defeated and to not give up. I realize now that my faith became strong during those years and I gained a genuine compassion for the sick.

I thank God for giving me a solution to my problems after ten years. I wanted it to be sooner, but our times are in His hands. Now I'm doing great, and it's wonderful to do what I do and feel good! But many times I had to say, "I would rather do my job and feel good, but hear this devil: I will do it, whether I feel good or not."

While I was suffering, I had to speak words of determination out loud: "I would rather feel good while I do this. Doing it this way is hard, but I am going to fulfill God's call on my life no matter how I feel. I'll do everything God wants me to do and be all He wants me to be!" I remember one morning when I felt really bad. I barely had any strength, but I prayed and told the Lord, "I may not have much strength, but whatever I do have I will use it to serve You the rest of my life." Each time I made a decision like that one, the devil was losing and God was winning.

The primary reason I was so determined to obey God's will whether I felt well physically or not was that I love God. I also knew I would be miserable if I tried to do anything less than everything God called me to do. You may not always want to make the effort to be determined, but I guarantee that you do not want to risk being outside God's will simply because you will not commit to doing everything required to obey it.

Settle the Dispute

Remember, the definition of *determine* carries the idea of settling a dispute. This is important because if you are going to commit to anything, you will have to settle the never-ending dispute between your flesh and your spirit. I often say the flesh is a "gambler," but the spirit is an "investor." As you follow the Holy Spirit and His leading in your heart (your spirit), you will invest in tomorrow by making right choices today.

Galatians 5:17 says, "For the desires of the flesh are opposed to the [Holy] Spirit and the [desires of the] Spirit are opposed to the flesh (godless human nature); for these are antagonistic to each other [continually withstanding and in conflict with each other]." This verse is basically telling us a war rages within us all the time. The flesh and the spirit do not ever get along; they always fight against each other.

This happens in all of us. We have a desire, an impulse, or a sense about something, and we know in our hearts it is right. But our minds try to talk us out of acting on it. Let's say you sense you are to give some money to a family in need. Your heart believes it is the right thing to do, and you believe it will please God and is even inspired by His Spirit. Your flesh will say, "You should not give away that money. You know you need it" or "Don't give anything to those people, they have never done anything for you." The flesh rages against the spirit, and you begin trying to figure out which one to listen to.

I am convinced we miss many blessings in our lives because we try to understand so much instead of simply allowing the Holy Spirit to lead us. We need to settle the dispute between the flesh and the spirit and be determined to obey God, no matter what.

WAITING ON THE LORD

God compares His people to eagles: "But those who wait for the Lord [who expect, look for, and hope in Him] shall change and renew their strength and power; they shall lift their wings and mount up [close to God] as eagles [mount up to the sun]; they shall run and not be weary, they shall walk and not faint or become tired" (Isaiah 40:31). I believe God chose to liken us to eagles to motivate us to rise to our potential in life and to encourage us to wait on Him and find our strength in Him. When success does not come easily, when we find ourselves frustrated and weary in our efforts, we need to wait for the Lord.

What does it really mean to wait for the Lord? It simply means spending time with Him, being in His presence, meditating on His Word, worshipping Him, keeping Him at the center of our lives. One meaning of the word *wait* is "to be twisted or braided together." If we think about a braid in someone's hair, we realize that the hair is woven together so that we cannot tell where one strand ends and another begins. That is the way God wants us to be in our union with Him—so intimately intertwined and tightly woven together with Him that we are truly one with Him, that we are direct representatives of His character. As we wait on Him, we become more and more like Him. Waiting is not passive; it is very active spiritually.

> *Waiting is not passive; it is very active spiritually.*

While we wait, we need to aggressively expect God to do great things in us and in our lives.

An intimate relationship with God will strengthen you in the innermost part of your being. It will strengthen your heart; it will carry you through the hard times in your life with a sense of peace and confidence that all is well, no matter what is happening. It will give you the strength to endure tough situations in such a way that many of the people around you may not even be able to detect even the slightest stress in your life. When you wait on the Lord in the way I describe, you draw everything you need from Him. He is your refuge, your enabler, your joy, your peace, your righteousness, your hope. He gives you everything you need to live in victory over any circumstance.

Isaiah promises that when we wait on God and spend time with Him, becoming more like He is, we will renew our strength. That little prefix *re* means "to go back again, to be made new, to go back to the beginning of something." When we wait on God, our strength is made new again; we can fly as eagles do, over the storms of life; we can walk and run and not faint. We can approach a situation in which we have grown weary with fresh energy and passion. We are encouraged, energized, and less likely to want to give up when success eludes us.

One reason eagles symbolize strength is that they know how to make their strength work for them. They don't expend their energy needlessly. Just as these magnificent birds know how to allow the thermal currents of the physical world to carry them, "eagle Christians" understand the currents of the Holy Spirit. They perceive the moving of the Spirit and can flow through life easily, without strain, striving, and undue stress. This comes from waiting on God and enables them to go through life with strength, power, and vitality.

People often ask me, "How can you and Dave do what you do at your age?" The truth is, we probably feel better than many of the thirty-year-olds in our audiences. One reason for this is that we take care of ourselves physically. We eat healthily; we exercise; we drink plenty of water; and we get enough sleep. We strive to keep excess stress out of our lives and we have learned to wait on the Lord. Jesus said that the weary, the worn out, and the exhausted should come to Him (see Matthew 11:28) and He would cause them to rest.

Many times, between speaking sessions at our conferences, I lie on the bed in my hotel room and rest my body. I also use that time just talking to the Lord. I don't say anything fancy, just, "I love You, Lord; I need You. Help me tonight. Thanks for what You did today." In those moments, I am not only resting my physical body, I am also resting spiritually by trusting God to be my helper and my strength.

Sometimes I grow weary—not just physically, but in other ways too, and need more than a quick rest. When that happens, I spend a day or two being alone as much as possible. I just want to go somewhere with my coffee and sit in a chair and be quiet. I want to spend quiet time with God, and I know that time with Him will renew my strength.

No one is exempt from the need for renewal; everyone needs times of rest, refreshing, and restoration. As you go through life, you grow weary. As you experience disappointments, you grow weary. As you work to meet deadlines and budgets and quotas, you grow weary. As you study for exams, you grow weary.

When weariness sets in, bad situations can arise. Weary people often make comments without thinking, take shortcuts they later regret, and settle for less than the best because they are tired of waiting. Weary people are being unwise if they do not allow their strength to be renewed. I believe many people make poor decisions because they become worn and fail to take the time to draw close to God and wait on Him so they can be strengthened and restored.

I'm convinced that people would make better choices in life if they would simply spend time with God on a regular basis. If they will seek God, they will hear from Him. Many times, they may not even realize He is speaking, but they will find themselves knowing what to do and what not to do in certain situations.

Begin to take time to wait on God and allow Him to renew your strength so you can soar. Begin today to take breaks as soon as you feel weary and say, "I love You, Lord. I need You. I feel a little weary, Lord. Strengthen me."

> *Take time to wait on God and allow Him to renew your strength so you can soar.*

You may not be able to go on a two-week vacation right now, but you can start with several five-minute vacations each day. You may not be able to go away for several days, but even if you have to escape to a bathroom stall or play a worship song in your car, get alone with God for a few minutes and say, "Jesus, I need a little renewal. I love You. I worship You. Strengthen me and renew me." He wants to strengthen and restore you so you will be able to persevere and enjoy success. Waiting on the Lord does not have to be complicated. Just put Him at the top of your priority list. He wants you to have and enjoy a quality of life you may be missing because you are not spending time with Him.

RENEWAL

Psalm 103:2–5 says:

> *Bless . . . the Lord, O my soul, and forget not [one of] all His benefits—Who forgives [every one of] all your iniquities, Who heals [each one of] all your diseases, Who redeems your life from the pit and corruption, Who beautifies, dignifies, and crowns you with loving-kindness and tender mercy; Who satisfies your mouth [your necessity and desire at your personal age and situation] with good so that your youth, renewed, is like the eagle's [strong, overcoming, soaring]!* (*emphasis mine*).

Most of us find the idea of having our youth renewed very appealing. We'd like to look younger and have the kind of energy we had in our earlier days. But I believe that what the psalmist calls "youth" we refer to as "young at heart"—a fresh, vibrant approach to life, rather than a tired, jaded, negative outlook. Youth is not just a matter of chronological age; it's what goes on inside of you. You live in a body, but you are a spirit, and if you keep your spirit strong, it will affect your body, your mind, your emotions, and your decisions in positive ways.

The psalmist would not have mentioned having our youth renewed like the eagle's if the eagle did not teach us something about renewing youth. I find the eagle's renewal process fascinating and awesome, and I hope you will too.

The Process of Renewal

There comes a time in the eagle's life when he is not as quick as he once was. His takeoff is not as fast as it was years ago; he is slower in flight; his previously sharp talons have grown dull; calcifications have formed on his beak; his feathers have worn and now give off a telltale whistle when he dives for his prey. He's still an eagle, but he has lost much of his strength and prowess.

When this happens, the eagle settles onto a high rock as close to the sun as he possibly can and begins to pluck out his feathers one by one—sometimes as many as seven thousand of them. He's not nearly as concerned with the pain as with the progress. He then seeks a cool, refreshing stream in which to clean himself. The water washes away all the caked mud and dirt, parasites, and insects that may have collected on him over time. When he is fresh, clean, and practically naked, the eagle stands before the sun and begins to wait.

The regrowth he needs will take about forty days. During that time, he sharpens his talons and beak by rubbing them back and forth on a rock. He uses that same rock to beat the calcification off of his beak. Other eagles who have already been through this process may drop food to him. He goes through a quiet season of relative weakness, but then his strength is renewed.

I believe God wants us to learn something from this process the eagle endures. There are times we feel dry, weak, defeated, and discouraged. There are times when life deals us bitter blows and our dreams crumble right before our eyes, when someone we love hurts us, when someone we trust betrays us, when we really thought something was finally going to work out and did not. These are the kinds of situations that make us want to quit. During those times, we really need to be renewed. If we don't take time for renewal, we are in danger of reacting to our circumstances emotionally, which always means responding without wisdom and often contributes to making bad situations even worse.

These are the times we really have to get serious with God. We need more than we usually get from our daily devotional routines. Some people may need to take a lesson from the eagle and set aside a forty-day period of prayer and fasting, seeking God, worshipping Him, and pouring out their hearts to Him. To those who have never fasted this may sound extreme, but desperate people do desperate things in desperate times. Other people need to get *radical* about bringing peace into their lives—turning off the television for a while or turning off their cell phones at a certain time each evening. Maybe you need time to examine your life to decide what is not bearing fruit and needs to be cut off.

I'm convinced that we all need extended or intense times of restoration and renewal. Personally, I try to schedule three or four each year to get away by myself for a week. I make the effort to take these times away, because I believe one of the best gifts we can give ourselves is time alone with God.

We need times of real quiet because we can connect with God in awesome ways in those

> *One of the best gifts we can give ourselves is time alone with God.*

places of deep peace and quiet. We do not have to feel we have had a definite "word" from God, nor do we need to have a supernatural experience. Honoring God by giving Him special, set-apart time will produce great results in our lives and bring restoration and refreshment. We will find ourselves making better decisions, displaying godly character with ease, and enjoying all of life much more. Time is one of the most important things we can give God. It tells Him He is important to us and that we realize we cannot manage life properly without Him.

In your pursuit of success, remember to be committed and determined, and wait on the Lord and renew your strength. As you do, you will be empowered to keep going without giving up.

A Voice in the Wilderness

No stranger to hardship or persecution, Marian Anderson was born in 1897, in the "Negro Quarter" of Philadelphia, to a loving family with very limited financial resources. When her father died unexpectedly when she was only ten, money was tight, and her mother went to work as a cleaning woman and a laundress to support Marian and her two sisters.

Marian's amazing singing ability made a way for her to enjoy opportunities otherwise unavailable to her. She began singing in the choir of the Union Baptist Church, where people quickly noticed the quality, range, and richness of her remarkable voice. They knew it was something special. They also knew Marian's family could not afford formal vocal training for her, so the church sponsored a benefit concert, with ten-year-old Marian as the featured soloist, to pay for her voice lessons.

Her family couldn't afford piano lessons either, so she taught herself to play. When she wanted to learn to play the violin, she took a job scrubbing steps to make money to buy her own instrument. Obviously, she was fiercely committed to her music. At one point, she went to apply for admission to a music school in Philadelphia and was treated rudely by a young receptionist. When Marian expressed her desire to pursue enrollment, the young woman replied, "We don't take colored."

At the age of nineteen Marian was introduced to well-known voice teacher Giuseppe Boghetti, who was her teacher, coach, and friend for years. As her abilities and exposure grew, she began receiving invitations to sing and even to tour. With her confidence strong and with strong supporters around her, she arranged to sing at New York's town hall in 1924. The concert was so poorly attended and so negatively reviewed that she considered abandoning music altogether.

But Marian soon bounced back. She went on to win a voice competition sponsored by the Philadelphia Philharmonic Society and then to triumph over more than three hundred other contestants in the Lewisohn Stadium competition. She began touring again, and in 1928, she sang a solo recital at Carnegie Hall.

In 1939, despite her remarkable accomplishments, Anderson was still denied opportunities because of racism. That year, the owners of Washington DC's Constitution Hall refused to allow her to sing because of her race. When Eleanor Roosevelt, wife of the president of the United States, heard what had happened, she made arrangements for Marian to sing at the Lincoln Memorial instead. Approximately seventy-five thousand people attended that outdoor concert. That event was a significant moment in the advancement of civil rights in America and gave many other people who suffered from racism and injustice the courage to pursue their dreams.

Anderson went on to become the first African American to appear as a soloist at New York's Metropolitan Opera. She also sang at inauguration ceremonies and received many prestigious awards, including the Presidential Medal of Freedom in 1963 and a Grammy Award for Lifetime Achievement in 1991. As her outstanding career drew to a close, she launched her 1956 farewell tour with a triumphant concert at a place that once refused to even allow her inside its doors—Constitution Hall in Washington DC.

No matter what doors seem closed to you today, keep going and never give up. Persevere with determination, and opportunities that seem impossible today will open for you tomorrow.

CHAPTER 9

OVERCOMING THE OBSTACLES TO SUCCESS

"When you get into a tight place and everything goes against you, till it seems as though you could not hold on a minute longer, never give up then, for that is just the place and time that the tide will turn."

HARRIET BEECHER STOWE

A donkey fell into a deep well, and the farmer who owned him had no idea how to get the donkey out. After much thought, he concluded the best solution would be to call some of his friends to help bury the donkey in the well. After all, he reasoned, the donkey was old and trying to get him out of the well was going to be a lot of trouble.

The neighboring farmers arrived with the shovels and they all began to pitch dirt into the well, on top of the donkey. The donkey began to make horrible noises—for a while. Then the donkey was silent. The men peered down into the well and saw an amazing sight.

Every time they threw a shovel full of dirt into the well, the donkey simply shook it off, so it ended up under his feet instead of on top of him. They kept shoveling, trying to bury the helpless donkey and he kept shaking off the dirt! Before long, the pile of dirt with which they were trying to bury him became tall enough to raise him out of the well, and he simply stepped off of the pile onto level ground.

If the donkey had just stood there and allowed the dirt to bury him, he would not have survived. But he was determined to get out of that pit. Every time a shovel full of dirt landed on him, he shook it off and climbed on top of it.

I want you to be like the donkey. Use the difficulties and obstacles you face as stepping-stones to your goals in life. When a seemingly impossible situation comes your way, do not just allow it to bury you. Be creative about overcoming it and determined to make it work for you, not against you. Turn it to your favor, even if you have to get on top of it one step at a time. Let the circumstances that could suffocate you be the very situations that strengthen you and raise you to a new level. Be a person who is willing to work with God to develop a determined, "can do" attitude; act on the truth that His power is at work within you and that you can do all things through Christ who strengthens you (see Philippians 4:13), no matter what stands in your way.

CERTAIN TO SUCCEED

True success does not come easily or without hurdles for anyone. It is the result of hard work, patience, determination, creativity, sacrifice, and moving beyond mistakes—but it does come. The only way you will ever be a failure is to give up, and you'll be most tempted to do so when you face opposition.

Scripture clearly teaches us we have an enemy who wants to frustrate and defeat us. His primary goals are to "steal and kill and destroy" us (John 10:10), and he spends his time roaming around "like a lion roaring [in fierce hunger], seeking someone to seize upon and devour" (1 Peter 5:8). He will oppose and interfere with our success in every possible way, doing his best to discourage us so we will give up.

I want you to be successful in every area of your life—your work, your relationships, your marriage, your parenting, your finances, your health, your ministry, your creative expressions, your pursuit of God's plans, and everything else in which you are involved. But I know lasting success requires effort, and as you work toward it, the enemy will be there to try to steal, kill, or destroy it. It's crucial to learn to keep moving forward in strength when success does not come as easily as you would like and when you face the obstacles you are sure to encounter along the way.

CLEARING HURDLE #1: THE TEMPTATION TO QUIT

The temptation to quit is part of being human, but giving in to it is equal to giving up. We do not avoid the temptation by sitting still and refusing to deal with it or wishing God would remove it. It's one of the realities of the Christian life and a hindrance to success we must work to overcome. The Bible tells us in Luke 22:40, "Pray that you may not [at all] enter into temptation." Tempting believers is part of the devil's job. As long as we live, we'll be tempted; and as long as we follow Jesus, our job is to resist temptations.

> *Tempting believers is part of the devil's job. As long as we live, we'll be tempted; and as long as we follow Jesus, our job is to resist temptations.*

Because we don't always realize that feelings of discouragement and thoughts of quitting are from the enemy, we don't always resist such temptations as we should. Some thoughts the enemy may plant in your mind to tempt you to give up might sound like this:

- This is too difficult. It will require too much effort.
- I really am not qualified to do this.
- I am facing too many problems and can't possibly solve them all.

- I have no one to help me.
- My friends and family think I'm crazy for pursuing this.
- This will require too much of a sacrifice.
- I don't have the money to do this.
- I'll never be able to finish this.
- What was I thinking when I agreed to this assignment?
- I knew this would never work.
- I need to go back to my old job/city/way of life/ministry. Everything was better there.

I encourage you to begin to recognize temptations to quit as works of the enemy; and I want you to start resisting each temptation with everything in you. Don't flirt with temptation or consider any temptation insignificant. Don't let the devil lure you into passivity or wait until you've been in a depressed, hopeless slump for three days, listening to the enemy list reasons to abandon your cause. Resist the devil at his onset! Declare war against temptation. Show the enemy no mercy. The *instant* you feel tempted to give up, you need to say aloud, "*I will not quit.* I *refuse* to give up. I *will* finish what God has called me to do."

In over thirty years of ministry, I've often been tempted to quit, especially during the early years when we traveled extensively. There were many occasions when I woke up in hotel rooms, exhausted from preaching the previous night and weary of hearing about problems at the office—someone quit; an urgent matter needed my attention; we received a bill we weren't expecting; and so on. At times I became extremely discouraged, sometimes to the point of tears. I didn't always want to get dressed and go preach to people about pressing through their difficulties when I felt overwhelmed by the pressures in my own life.

Over the years, I've had to resist many temptations to want to give up, and I've learned the best way to work at resisting temptation is to do your job in prayer. It's far wiser and more effective to pray and ask for God's help as you stand against temptation than to try to exert willpower alone. When you seek His strength, He gives it to you.

Jesus told the disciples twice in one day to pray that they wouldn't enter into temptation. If it was that serious a threat in His eyes, we'd better take it seriously too. Look at Luke 22:40 and the verses following: "And when He came to the place, He said to them, Pray that you may not [at all] enter into temptation....And when He got up from prayer, He came to the disciples and found them sleeping from grief, and He said to them, Why do you sleep? Get up and pray that you may not enter [at all] into temptation" (Luke 22:40, 45–46).

Be sure that you work with God and pray that you won't surrender to the temptation to give up. Ask Him to help you finish what He has called you to do, be all He wants you to be, do all He wants you to do, and have all He wants you to have.

CLEARING HURDLE #2: PERSONAL PROBLEMS

When the enemy sees we are determined to complete an assignment from God, one of his favorite and most effective tools to make us give up is personal pain. I've seen so many people who face personal crises and problems as they walk through life, and I've experienced personal pain myself as I've headed toward the accomplishment of goals or the fulfillment of dreams.

I once had to conduct a seminar during a time when I was really heartbroken over a serious situation involving one of our children. The place where I was speaking had a small room behind the platform, a nice place for speakers to take breaks and be refreshed between speaking sessions. When the time came for me to speak, I would walk onto the platform and conduct the meeting as usual. Then I would go behind the platform and cry. When the next session began, I dried my tears and carried out my responsibilities again; then I went back to that little room and cried some more. I repeated that cycle for the duration of the seminar. I was hurting personally, but I still fulfilled my responsibility.

To be people who remain determined and diligent, we must learn how to make it through times of personal pain. People of character simply don't say, "Well, I'm not going to do my job tonight because I have a problem! I'm going through a personal crisis, so how could people expect me to minister to them?"

That may sound silly to you, but there are people who allow their personal problems to rule their lives and dictate which commitments they keep and which ones they cancel. If they have personal problems, they decide they can't work in the church nursery on their assigned Sunday. They don't want to do their jobs or keep their word. They fail to do what they said they would do because they think their individual crises should excuse them from their commitments.

Helping someone when you're struggling with pain of a personal nature is extremely difficult; it takes commitment and determination. As a minister, I can assure you, ministering to hurting people when you are hurting too is quite a challenge. Listening to other people's problems when you have problems of your own can be extremely hard. But it helps you develop great compassion and it makes you stronger.

When you're suffering, you still need to keep your word if at all possible and do your best to help others. In fact, those are precisely the seasons when you need to be diligent to keep your commitments and actively look for ways to bless the people around you. Times of personal testing are exactly the times you *need* to go all the way through what you promised God and keep serving Him.

We all experience personal problems, and there are times in life when it is impossible for us to keep a commitment, but we should do our best to keep those times to a minimum. Our challenges may pertain to our health, our children, our marriages, aging parents, stress at work, time management—and the list goes on. We cannot allow these difficult circumstances to derail us as we head toward fulfilling God's plan for our lives. The people who refuse to be deterred are the ones who are determined to stay focused on their jobs, who stay devoted to God, who remain committed to their families, who are determined to confront every obstacle that comes their way. They are winners in life.

CLEARING HURDLE #3: REJECTION

When people reject you, you may not want to keep doing what you're supposed to do; you may want to find a place to hide and nurse your wounds, but don't! Keep moving forward, no matter who disapproves or tries to stop you.

If you look back over the course of your life, you'll probably find that every time God has tried to take you to a new level, someone usually disapproved. In some way, that person sent you the message "If you do this, I'm not going to be your friend." Do you know why this happens so often? Probably more than anything, Satan uses the pain of rejection from other people to keep us from pursuing God's will. The pain of being rejected by those we love is so powerful it often causes us to abandon our determination to do what God has called us to do. Rejection causes us to convince ourselves we cannot do anything to please anybody and makes us want to give up. We need to remember that we may not please people all the time, but if we please God, that is what really matters.

Jesus dealt with the issue of rejection in Matthew 10:5–14. In this passage, He warned His disciples that some people would reject them, and He told them how to handle that rejection: "And whoever will not receive and accept and welcome you nor listen to your message, as you leave that house or town, shake the dust [of it] from your feet" (v. 14). In a very real sense, they were to "shake off" the rejection and go on.

When God filled me with the Holy Spirit, He was equipping me for the call He was about to release in my life—to begin teaching His Word.

As soon as that happened, I experienced quite a bit of rejection, which I mentioned earlier. Almost every friend I had thought I was crazy. At that time, in the circles in which I moved, women did not preach and teach the Bible. When everyone around me seemed to reject me, I had to be determined to not give up on what God called me to do.

Many people will want to attach themselves to you when you are going "up" in life—when you are doing something others think is good or when you are gaining visibility, prestige, or respect. But when you do something unpopular or out of the ordinary, you may lose some friends. If you want to do anything great for God, you may have to be willing to endure rejection and loneliness for a while. It is worth it, though, and in the end, you will be glad that you pressed through. Realize that no matter how much rejection you face, God accepts you completely. He wants you to break through the barrier of rejections and keep making progress toward your goals.

CLEARING HURDLE #4: WANTING TOO MUCH TOO SOON

People have asked me through the years, "What has been the most difficult aspect or experience of your ministry?" I always respond, "Not giving up when we were laying the foundation." Though we have certainly faced our share of situations that tempted us to want to give up, nothing has been as challenging as staying focused and diligent during those early years, when so much of the ministry was unseen and unknown. We certainly wanted a fruitful ministry, but we knew we needed a strong foundation before we could build one. That meant everything needed to be done with excellence.

Dave and I were growing personally at the same time we were trying to grow the ministry God had called us to. He spoke to our hearts about excellence, integrity, and keeping all strife out of our personal lives and ministry. We were being stretched like never before. Dave and I were learning how to work together, and keeping strife out of our personal relationship was something we both had to work hard to achieve.

We didn't have many people to help us and we had no experience, so everything we did was a huge step of faith. Every decision seemed major to us and we were learning how to hear from God. It was often tiring and discouraging, especially when we did our best and the growth was painfully slow.

I began by teaching a Bible study in my living room for five years. For the last half of that time period, God added a second Bible study in someone else's home, so I taught two Bible studies per week, with approximately twenty-five or thirty people in each one. I also did other types of ministry—counseling, helping people gain freedom from various types of bondage, passing out evangelistic tracts on downtown streets, praying (a lot)—anything I could do to serve God. I had quit my job in order to minister to others and, although we struggled with finances, God gave us the grace to not give up.

After five years, God promoted me. I went to work at a church in St. Louis, and I worked there for five years. My first paycheck was sixty-five dollars and that seemed like a fortune to me. There, I started a women's meeting. God's hand was upon that gathering; it grew very quickly and we soon had about five hundred ladies attending each week.

Over time, I became an associate pastor in that church and then went on to teach at the church's Bible college. Little by little, God trained me and strengthened me, but I often wanted more.

The time came when God spoke to my heart and said, *Now I'm finished with your work in this church. Take your ministry, and go north, south, east, and west.* As I obeyed that word, which took time, I found myself with more meetings than I had held before, but they were smaller in size. I felt as though I was starting all over again! I was ministering to more people, but they were in smaller groups—seventy-five in one place, sixty in another, one hundred over here, eighty-five over there. When we had meetings of one hundred and fifty or two hundred people, we thought we were really doing something! I was working harder than ever and had more responsibility.

Each year, the ministry grew and our meetings became larger and larger. We reached three hundred, then four hundred, then four hundred and fifty. By that time we were becoming known and beginning to travel to hold meetings in other cities. And then the growth stopped—at least for a season.

But one morning while Dave was getting ready for work, the Spirit of God visited him in a powerful way and he began to weep. God showed him the condition in which many people live and said to Dave, *All these years I've prepared you to go on television. Now I want you to go on television. It's time for this ministry to go on television. You have the answers people need.* We had those answers because God had used the times of slow growth to teach us what He wanted us to share with others.

When we went on television, our ministry tripled in three months. Since then, it has grown so quickly we've been running to keep up with God. We now have more people on staff than used to attend my meetings. We have great vision and plans for the future, and I can honestly say God has caused our ministry to grow in exactly the right way and at precisely the right times. I'm glad He has led us as patiently as He has, even though I grew frustrated at times.

Whatever you believe God wants to do in your life, be patient as He brings it to pass. Eagerly embrace the times of teaching and preparation He takes you through, even when it seems painfully slow. Don't long for too much too fast, but be thankful every day that God is bringing growth, expansion, and new opportunities your way in His perfect timing.

CLEARING HURDLE #5: INCONVENIENCE

We live in an "instant" society. We want everything to be easy, comfortable, and convenient. When faced with a little work we say, "Oh, woe is me. That's too hard. I have to unload the dishwasher." I was around before dishwashers existed and all I have to say to those who complain about dishwashers is, be thankful you didn't have to wash the dishes by hand! And you didn't have to dry them!

We have escalators and elevators so we don't have to climb stairs. We have push-button microwaves so we can cook our food in seconds, so we will not miss our favorite television programs. We have instant potato flakes so we do not have to peel, boil, and mash our potatoes. We have drive-through windows so we don't have to get out of our cars for our prescriptions, dry cleaning, or tacos. We have push-button this and push-button that, and instant this and instant that. We are addicted to ease and comfort.

The sad part about all these conveniences is, although we view them as "good," they actually work against us in many ways. They cause us to seek the easy way out when taking the more difficult way just might build something of worth in us. You will never face an obstacle God is not aware of. When your journey becomes difficult, remember that even though the world prefers "the easy road," God did not build you for comfort. He designed and equipped you for adversity, whether you know it or not. He made you in such a way that the best comes out of you when you face hard situations and you experience joy and strength when you overcome them.

CLEARING HURDLE #6: JEALOUSY

Years ago, Dave and I both smoked cigarettes, and God was dealing with us about quitting. It was not good for our health, and it was an expensive, stinky habit. Dave simply said to God, "Well, I know I need to stop smoking, but I am going to continue as I am until You give me the grace to quit. I'm not going to worry about it; I cast my care on You." The next day, he got up not wanting to smoke, and to this day, he has never wanted another cigarette.

Do you think I was able to stop smoking as easily as Dave was? No! Let me repeat: *No!* I had to *suffer!* I tried to quit so many times I lost count. My routine of "walking it out" went something like this: I couldn't stand to be without a cigarette, so I went and bought a pack. Then I reminded myself I was quitting, so I threw it away. Then I reached the point where I had to have a cigarette, so I rummaged through the trash can to find one! Then I felt terrible about smoking, so I put out the cigarette and threw it away again. And in the middle of the night I would dig it out and relight it! There I was, in the wee hours of the morning, puffing on a cigarette under the biggest load of condemnation you can imagine!

At that time, Dave and I attended a Spirit-filled church and after services, I would make a beeline to the parking lot, roll down my car windows, lie down in the car, and smoke a cigarette—and I thought none of our church friends knew. They probably thought our car was on fire because of the smoke rolling out of the windows.

All this time, Dave was going through life smoke-free. Many times I asked, "Dave, isn't this *hard* for you?"

"Oh no," he responded. "God's grace is on me."

Furious and wanting a cigarette, I wanted to scream, "Well, where is His grace for *me?!*" Perhaps I didn't have enough faith at the time to receive His grace for me, but whatever the problem was I kept smoking and resented Dave because quitting had been so easy for him.

Since that time, I've learned that one obstacle to experiencing the breakthroughs we long for is the tendency to look at others and become jealous of the way God brought breakthrough in their lives. We think something is unfair about the fact that they enjoyed quick success, seemingly without effort, while we have to struggle and suffer. Part of overcoming the obstacle of jealousy is trusting God enough to believe that His plan for each of us is perfect. It may not seem fair at times, but God does know what He is doing and He knows how He wants to use us in the future.

In my case, I finally got determined and said with much prayer and leaning on God, "I am going to quit smoking! With God's help I *will* quit smoking! I do not care how hard it is, *I am going to quit!*" After that, I went through a difficult period for about thirty days and then it was over. I finally had a breakthrough and have never smoked or wanted to smoke again.

Why didn't God deliver me the easy way like He did Dave? I don't know. But I do know that I learned an important lesson about trusting His timing for me without being jealous of the way He works for others.

CLEARING HURDLE #7: SELFISHNESS

Another obstacle to the pursuit of our goals is the fact that we can be selfish, especially with our personal space and our freedom. If we're going to be committed to never giving up, we're going to have to sacrifice our selfish wants at times. Persistence and determination are hard on the "self." After all, if I'm committed to something, then what happens when the time comes and I don't feel like doing it? We often think freedom is being able to do whatever we want to, whenever we want to do it. But the truth is, if we ever could live that way, it would just drive us to be more and more selfish and self-centered.

If we aren't determined to never give up, it's easy for the devil to talk us out of doing whatever we should be doing by appealing to our selfish desires. Persistence requires us to discipline our feelings and do what is right, no matter how we feel about it.

We need to surrender our freedom and our personal space once in a while and learn to say no to ourselves. We cannot trust our flesh; it won't get us where we need to be when we need to be there. It will want to stop when we need to keep pressing on. It will tempt us with our personal space and freedom—at the expense of our personal growth.

It says that feeling good right now is more valuable than living a disciplined, committed lifestyle that will result in the achievement of our goals and the fulfillment of our destinies.

We need to surrender our freedom and our personal space once in a while and learn to say no to ourselves.

Not only does God want you to succeed, He *created* you to succeed. And He does not want you to settle for anything less. Don't allow failures or mistakes to cause you to give up; let them teach you what to avoid the next time around. As you move toward success, wait on the Lord and let Him renew your strength. Success will not come easily, but it *will* come, if you persevere.

The Freedom Fighter

British political leader William Wilberforce is one of the world's best-known champions of freedom and opponents of cruelty and injustice. In 1780, this Cambridge-educated son of a wealthy merchant became a member of Parliament when he was twenty-one years old, the youngest age permitted. A charming and articulate speaker, Wilberforce enjoyed representing his constituency in Parliament, but did not align himself with any particular cause or legislative agenda during his early years.

In 1785, Wilberforce had what can only be called a remarkable encounter with God. After that, he wanted to do everything he could do to serve God and thought he had to choose between his political career and full-time ministry. Eventually, he realized he didn't have to be a professional minister to do God's work, but that he could do God's work most effectively outside the walls of a church, in the halls of government.

By 1787, Wilberforce had emerged as Parliament's dominant voice against the slave trade. He had very few supporters, because the wealth of the British Empire depended on slave labor and Britain led the world in taking slaves from Africa and shipping them under horrific conditions to docks where they were sold like livestock to plantation owners and then forced into manual labor and often treated terribly.

Speaking of the slave trade, Wilberforce said: "Let the policy be what it might, let the consequences be what they would, I am from this time determined that I would never rest until I have affected its abolition." Wilberforce certainly did not rest in his efforts. He endured sickness, hardship, controversy, the betrayal of colleagues he believed supported him, and the mockery of others, as he tirelessly and passionately worked to stop human trafficking. He presented his bill for the abolition of the slave trade to Parliament eighteen times before it finally passed.

In 1807, Wilberforce finally saw the goal for which he had labored, sacrificed, and endured ridicule accomplished. The slave trade was officially abolished. However, the end of the slave trade did not liberate people who were already enslaved, so that became Wilberforce's next objective. Wilberforce died in 1833, knowing the end of slavery was imminent. One month after his death, the law abolishing slavery was enacted.

Injustice continues to run rampant in the world today. You may or may not be called to publicly champion a specific cause, as Wilberforce was, but you can treat people well, stand up for what is right in your life, and help those who cannot stand up for themselves. Like Wilberforce, you can serve God wherever you are—as a university student, a businessperson, a stay-at-home mother, a medical or legal professional, or whatever you do. Be a person who knows what is right, according to the Word of God, and who never gives up in your efforts to see right prevail.

CHAPTER 10

TESTIMONY BEGINS WITH T-E-S-T

"Accept the challenges so that you may feel
the exhilaration of victory."
GENERAL GEORGE S. PATTON

I'm sure you know people with amazing stories of the way God has worked in their lives. I always love to hear a great testimony, but I also know that behind every extraordinary account of someone's life lies some kind of challenge or difficulty. No one ever has a testimony without a test.

We must pass all kinds of tests as we go through our lives, and passing them is part of never giving up. It's vital for us to understand the important role that tests and trials play in our lives, because understanding them helps us endure them and actually be strengthened by them. Everything God permits us to go through will ultimately be good for us—no matter how much it hurts, how unfair it is, or how difficult it is. When we encounter tests and trials, if we will embrace them and refuse to run from them, we will learn some lessons that will help us in the future and become stronger.

> *It's vital for us to understand the important role that tests and trials play in our lives.*

In this chapter, I want us to

explore five of the most common, most important tests we must pass in life.

TRIALS AND TESTS

Trials "try" us, and tests "test" us. Most of the time, the purpose of them is to show us who we really are, to reveal character in us. We can think all kinds of good thoughts about ourselves, but until we are put to the test, we don't know whether those things have become realities in us or not. We may consider ourselves generous, honest, or deeply committed to a particular truth or ideal, but the depth of these dynamics only reveals itself when we're under pressure.

We never know what we really believe until our beliefs are tested. We never know how godly we are until our faith is tried. We can't predict how we will behave under pressure until the stress hits an all-time high. We don't know whether we really are nice people until we have to be kind to someone when we don't feel like it. When we go through tests, we learn whether or not we really have the character and commitment we think we have. I believe it's very important for us to really know ourselves; so tests are good for us because they affirm strengths and reveal weaknesses. Don't be afraid to face your weaknesses. God's strength is available specifically for our weaknesses.

> *Don't be afraid to face your weaknesses. God's strength is available specifically for our weaknesses.*

Why did Jesus—our perfect Jesus—have to go out into the wilderness so the devil could tempt Him for forty days and forty nights? God the Father already knew Jesus would not succumb to the temptation. I believe that, in His humanity, Jesus went into the wilderness to build His own confidence and to show the devil He would be faithful to His heavenly Father, no matter what.

Other people cannot always pray all your giants away; they cannot fight all your battles for you. Your pastor can only go so far with you, but then you have to take the ball and make the touchdown. Your best friend or work colleague can only pray you a certain amount of the way through, but sooner or later, you have to learn how to pray. You have to learn how to find your own scriptures. You have to learn how to stand your own ground. You have to get to the point where every single time you have a problem, the first place you run is to God. You get your answers and advice from Him, not from your pastor, your best friend, or the person who sits next to you at work.

First Peter 4:12 gives us great insight into the purpose of trials: "Beloved, do not be amazed and bewildered at the fiery ordeal which is taking place to test your quality, as though something strange (unusual and alien to you and your position) were befalling you."
One reason we must go through trials is to test our quality. Often, we find ourselves wishing we had the faith of Sister so-and-so. I can assure you, if she has a strong and vibrant faith, she did not develop it easily. Just as muscles are built through exercise, firm faith comes from the furnace of affliction.
Sometimes people say to me, "Oh, I wish I had the kind of ministry you have, Joyce." Well, I did not get it by wishing. These people were not around when I was feeling I couldn't hold on one more second, begging God to help me not to quit or give up. They don't know the tests and trials I've faced along the way.
No one who does anything worthwhile for God has traveled an easy road. Doing great things for God requires character, and character is developed by passing life's tests and staying faithful to Him through the trials.

> *No one who does anything worthwhile for God has traveled an easy road.*

After many years of tests and trials, I have become more steadfast and patient than I ever thought possible. I'm still growing in these areas, but circumstances do not move me the way they used to. James 1:2–3 says: "Consider it wholly joyful, my brethren, whenever you are enveloped in or encounter trials of any sort or fall into various temptations. Be assured and understand that the trial and proving of your faith bring out endurance and steadfastness and patience."

I must say that before my trials worked steadfastness and patience in my life, they brought out many other negative qualities, mindsets, and attitudes I didn't know I had. One reason God allows us to go through tests and trials is so the hidden things in our hearts can be exposed. Until they are exposed, we cannot do anything about them. But once we see them, we can begin to face them and ask God to help us. God does not allow us to go through difficult times because He likes to see us suffer; He allows us to walk through them so we will recognize our need for Him. Never be afraid of the truth, because it is the truth that makes us free (see John 8:32).

Look again at James 1:3. The point is that everything you go through ultimately does work out for your good because it makes you stronger and builds your endurance; it develops godly character; it helps you to know yourself and to be able to deal with things on an honest level with God and take care of them so you can go on.

The next time you encounter some sort of test or trial, determine to believe it is for your good. Say to God: "Okay, Lord, I believe this is going to work out well for me. It doesn't feel good. I don't like it at all. I don't understand it! It hurts! It doesn't seem fair! But I believe You will use it for my good." Placing your faith in God opens the door for Him to work miracles out of messes!

THE "GET OVER IT" TEST

Another test we all have to pass in life is the "get over being offended" test, which can also be called the "bitterness-resentment-unforgiveness" test. The only way to get over being offended is to forgive. The sooner you do it, the easier it will be. Don't let offense take root in your heart, because it will be more difficult to deal with if you do.

One of our first responses when someone hurts or offends us should be to pray: "God, I choose to believe the best. My feelings are hurt, but You can heal me. I refuse to be bitter; I refuse to be angry; I refuse to be offended." You need to say with your mouth that you will not be offended because offense is a trap! It's the bait of Satan. He uses offenses to pull us away from God and His principles.

The word *offense* comes from the Greek word *skandalon*. A skandalon was the part of an animal trap that held the bait; its purpose was to lure a victim. Offense is the devil's bait to lure us into a trap of full-blown bitterness, resentment, and unforgiveness, so he can destroy our lives.

We Christians must learn to be good at forgiving people, because we will be doing it all of our lives. When we forgive, we are actually doing ourselves a favor. We are freeing ourselves from the agony of anger and bitter thoughts. As long as we live, we will encounter people who hurt us, reject us, disappoint us, use the wrong tone of voice with us, fail to understand us, or let us down in times of need. Those dynamics are part of human nature and they are part of the territory that comes with relationships. Why should we ruin our lives over other people's bad behavior? We need to take the high road and forgive!

> *We Christians must learn to be good at forgiving people, because we will be doing it all of our lives.*

Jesus knew this truth. That is why He responded as He did when Peter asked Him: "Lord, how many times may my brother sin against me and I forgive him and let it go? [As many as] up to seven times?" Jesus answered: "I tell you, not up to seven times, but seventy times seven!" (Matthew 18:21–22). What He meant was: "Forgive and keep on forgiving. Just keep it up, keep it up, keep it up, keep it up." Every time you decide to forgive, you are maintaining your freedom! You're refusing to be filled with negative thoughts and emotions and your decision enables God to release you from the trap of resentment.

We bless other people when we forgive them, but forgiveness is more for our benefit than for the benefit of those who hurt us. We extend forgiveness for ourselves because holding bitterness, resentment, and unforgiveness only hurts us. Most of the time, those who have offended us don't even realize what they have done and are not even aware we are suffering.

When people hurt or offend you, you may not be able to help the way you feel, but you can help what you do about it. If you are hurt, you are hurt; but God will heal your feelings if you will *by faith* obey His Word, pray for your enemies, and bless those who mistreat you (see Matthew 5:44). Turn the entire situation over to God and refuse to be offended.

I heard a story about a pastor I know. He was hosting a guest speaker in his church and the guest made critical remarks about the way the church handled their services. The guest preacher was young and inexperienced, and the pastor decided not to let his comments offend him. He sat in the front row of the church and repeated in a low whisper, "I will not get offended. I will not get offended." This story has stuck with me for a long time because it is an excellent example of someone who took quick action to make sure no root of offense or bitterness got into his heart.

Jesus tells us to bless those who hurt us (see Matthew 5:44), but how do we do that? One way is by not speaking negatively about them or telling others what they did to us. I believe we invite trouble into our lives when somebody does something wrong or hurtful to us and we tell other people about it for no reason except to gossip. When we hurt, we want sympathy, we tend to want people to know who hurt us and how it happened, but God does not want us to respond that way. He wants us to keep our mouths closed, to refuse to speak ill of others, and to pray for them and bless them. This is one way we overcome evil with good (see Romans 12:21)!

The Bible is full of stories of people who refused to be offended. Job was doubly blessed when he prayed for those who hurt him (see Job 42:10). Moses prayed for Miriam and Aaron right away when they judged him and came against him (see Numbers 12:13). You see, Moses was a godly man. When wronged, he fell on his face before God, saying basically, "Oh, God, oh, God, forgive them, forgive them, forgive them. They don't know what they're doing."

> *The next time someone hurts you, do yourself a favor and forgive quickly, refuse to be offended, and bless and pray for that person.*

The next time someone hurts you, do yourself a favor and forgive quickly, refuse to be offended, and bless and pray for that person. Do this over and over again. You will have many opportunities in life to pass the tests of offense, and I want you to pass with flying colors!

THE "JUDAS KISS" TEST

Judas was the disciple who betrayed Jesus with a kiss. He agreed to reveal who Jesus was for thirty pieces of silver, and said he would do it by kissing him, which was an acceptable greeting in Jesus' day. The "kiss" traditionally is a greeting of love and affection; therefore, the "Judas kiss" inflicts a deeper wound than ordinary offenses do. This kind of attack comes from someone with whom you have a close relationship, someone you love and trust. Many times a person who becomes a "Judas" in your life is someone you have helped and treated well.

There are many sad stories about pastors who have mentored young men in their congregations, taught them everything they know, given them opportunities to grow in their ministry gifts, and helped them earn respect, only to have these men leave their churches to start new ones, taking many of the members of the original church with them. This is an excellent example of a "Judas kiss." I believe such a situation is one of the worst tragedies that can happen to a church and one of the most painful situations a pastor can endure when he or she has invested his life in training an emerging leader.

What a sad turn of events we read about in Luke 22:48, when Judas betrayed Jesus with a kiss—a sign of love. It was not just anybody who betrayed Jesus; it was one of His twelve disciples; one of His close associates; one of His personal friends; someone to whom He gave a position of honor. Judas betrayed Jesus for *money* because he was greedy, so he *sold* Jesus for a few pieces of silver. And he did it with a kiss!

Being betrayed by someone you love is one of the hardest situations you will ever endure, but if it happens, you must let God heal you and move beyond it, or it will destroy you. You will simply be alone with your hurt, your resentment, and your pain. In addition, your ability to enjoy God and His good plan for you will be diminished, if not entirely destroyed. Do yourself a favor and totally forgive. God never asks us to do anything without giving us the ability to do it. You don't have to spend your life feeling hurt, bitter, angry, and offended. You can forgive and be free!

THE "MOTIVE" TEST

I like to define a motive as "the *why* behind the *what*." A motive is the reason we do what we do. We often say we are doing things for God, but sometimes we do not understand why we do them. We only know *what* we are doing, but we have not taken the time to truly understand what motivates us. Impure motives can cause many problems, one of which is being overcommitted, which results in unnecessary stress in our lives. Surely we won't live with extreme stress if we are obeying God and doing only what He wants us to do.

Never agree to do something in order to impress people or because you fear what they may think or say about you if you don't. God wants us to help and bless people, but a "good work" done with a wrong motive is no longer a good work. Don't say yes with your mouth if your heart is screaming no.

Take the motive test as often as you can. Begin to ask yourself questions that will help you assess your motives, such as:

- Why did I agree to serve on that committee? Am I looking for recognition?
- Why did I want to attend a certain function? Am I seeking social status?
- Why did I say I would lead the missions group at church? Do I really have a heart for evangelism and a longing to serve God, or do I want people to talk about what a good church member I am?
- Why do I really want that promotion at work so much? Is it motivated by God or worldly ambition?

As you evaluate your motives, you will begin to see what is in your heart. Pass the test by making sure your motives are pure and right before God. The motive test is a lifelong test. I frequently reevaluate my motives and discontinue things I find I am doing for the wrong reason, and that helps me keep my priorities in order.

THE "LOVING THE UNLOVELY" TEST

We all face the "loving the unlovely" test. When we ask God to teach us about love, we shouldn't expect Him to send us someone who is easy to love; that would not be much of a test. The test of loving those who are unlovely takes place when people come into our lives and affect us like sandpaper on our souls. These are the people who grate on our nerves, people we would rather not interact with. And yet, we know in our hearts God Himself has put these people in our lives.

Galatians 6:1–3 basically tells us how to pass the "loving the unlovely" test:

> Brethren, if any person is overtaken in misconduct or sin of any sort, you who are spiritual [who are responsive to and controlled by the Spirit] should set him right and restore and reinstate him, without any sense of superiority and with all gentleness, keeping an attentive eye on yourself, lest you should be tempted also. Bear (endure, carry) one another's burdens and troublesome moral faults, and in this way fulfill and observe perfectly the law of Christ (the Messiah) and complete what is lacking [in your obedience to it]. For if any person thinks himself to be somebody [too important to condescend to shoulder another's load] when he is nobody [of superiority except in his own estimation], he deceives and deludes and cheats himself.

This passage teaches us that when we are around people who are difficult to deal with, we will still treat them well and help restore them if we are truly spiritual. We won't make more out of their faults than necessary; and we will look for the good and not just the bad in them. We'll be concerned more about them than about how they're making us feel. Instead of judging them, we'll examine ourselves. We'll try to understand our weaknesses and ask God to help us rather than focusing on how much we think He needs to help those "unlovely" people. Loving those we consider unlovely is one of the most Christlike qualities we can develop.

THE "TEST OF TIME"

The final test to which I want to call your attention is the "test of time." Will you still be here—following God, obeying Him, living by His Word—five years from now? Will you still be doing everything

He has called you to do ten years from now? Will you walk with Him every day for the rest of your life, even through difficulties, and refuse to give up?

Let me encourage you as you think about passing the test of time: Make every effort to be on fire for God. Don't be passionate for Him for six months and then allow yourself to become lukewarm. Don't be disciplined one day and be lazy the next, or be diligent to live your life by the Word for one week and then ignore what God says a week later. Have staying power; be consistent over the course of time; be committed to God for the long haul. I have been serving God seriously for more than thirty years and I believe my greatest testimony is simply, "I'm still here!"

Whatever you may be facing right now, go ahead and go through it the right way so you won't have to go through it again. Remain stable in your attitudes and actions. Keep your commitments and continue reaching out in love to others who are hurting also.

In God's school, we never fail. We get to keep taking our tests over and over again until we pass them. I want you to pass your tests the first time so you don't have to waste the time I did in my life going around and around the same mountains. God's ways are always best, and the sooner we submit to them, the better our lives will be.

Not Your Average Cosmetic Change

Chances are, anytime you see a Cadillac in a certain shade of pink, you know what it means: the owner is a tremendously effective salesperson for Mary Kay cosmetics.

In 1963, the Mary Kay company had eleven salespeople. In 2007, it had more than 1.7 million sales representatives, called "Independent Beauty Consultants," in more than thirty countries around the world. What was the secret behind such phenomenal growth? A woman who never gave up, Mary Kay Ash.

She was born in 1918, in Hot Wells, Texas. By the time Mary Kay was six years old, she had the great responsibility of caring for a seriously ill relative while her mother worked, often more than fourteen hours per day, to provide for the family. Anytime Mary Kay faced a new or challenging situation, her mother told her "You can do it." Because of her mother's encouragement, she grew up feeling empowered, confident, and truly able to do anything.

As a young girl, Mary Kay wanted to grow up and become a doctor. In 1938, while studying to pursue that dream, she took a part-time sales job selling household goods for Stanley Home Products and quickly realized she was extremely talented as a salesperson. She soon chose business over medicine because she enjoyed such amazing success in sales.

Several years later, Ash went to work for a gift company, where she eventually became national training director. After twenty-five years as an outstanding employee in the area of direct sales, Ash resigned from the company because a man she had trained was promoted over her and received double the salary she was making.

But Mary Kay kept going. She realized she was not the only woman being treated unfairly in corporate environments, so

(continued)

she decided to write a book to help other women enjoy the opportunities that were not available to her. As she penned her thoughts, she realized she was not only offering women advice, she was writing the strategy and philosophy of a new company. She once said, "I envisioned a company in which any woman could become just as successful as she wanted to be. The doors would be wide open to opportunity for women who were willing to pay the price and had the courage to dream."

By 1963, she had a wealth of sales experience, a plan, five thousand dollars, and a twenty-year-old son to help her start her new business, called "Beauty by Mary Kay." According to the company Web site, "It was a first—a company dedicated to making life more beautiful for women. It was founded not on the competitive rule but on the Golden Rule—on praising people to success—and on the principle of placing faith first, family second and career third." Mary Kay often called it "a company with heart."

As a woman, Mary Kay had to struggle to achieve her full potential in the business world. Because she refused to give up, she was able to start an enormously successful company that would empower other women to do great things. I want to encourage you with a statement this innovative and determined businesswoman once made: "With your priorities in order, press on, and never look back."

CHAPTER 11

TRY SOMETHING NEW

*"You are never too old to set a new goal or to
dream a new dream."*

C. S. LEWIS

Someone once said, "Never be afraid to try something new. Remember, amateurs built the ark. Professionals built the *Titanic*." Sometimes we're tempted to give up because whatever we're doing doesn't work. When that happens, we have to try something new. As long as we're making progress in life, we will have new opportunities and face new challenges. We have dreams and goals that we want to pursue, but we also need solutions to the challenges that we experience along the way. If we know what to do, then we need to do it; if we don't, then we have the privilege of trusting God to guide us. The Bible says we are to do what the crisis demands and then stand firmly in our place (see Ephesians 6:13). Do what you can do and God will do what you cannot do.

As we continue learning to be determined and to not give up, we must understand how to embrace new things. Many times we say we want something new and then when new things come, they frighten us. New experiences and opportunities can be daunting, but they don't have to be. If we insist upon clinging to old methods, old ideas, old relationships, or old mind-sets and refuse to accept or embrace the new, we aren't going to progress in our lives. I want you to go forward—as far and as fast as God's will dictates—without giving up when you face a challenge that requires you to think or act in a new way. I believe God is doing a new thing in your life, and I want you to be ready to embrace it with passion.

You remember that God chose Joshua to succeed Moses as the leader of the Israelites and to take them into the Promised Land. God gave him the daunting task of leading an entire nation into a new place, a place where they'd never been before. They knew they were leaving behind a land of terrible oppression and hard labor as slaves in Egypt, and they heard they were headed to a land flowing with milk and honey, but they had never seen that land before. It was going to be new to them. Their story, even though it took place thousands of years ago, teaches us some important lessons about new experiences in our lives today.

In Joshua 3, we read that officers went through the Israelites' camp, "Commanding the people: When you see the ark of the covenant of the Lord your God being borne by the Levitical priests, set out from where you are and follow it" (v. 3).

The ark contained the Ten Commandments, which represent the will of God, and a piece of manna—the same manna with which God fed the Israelites in the wilderness for forty years. The manna represents God's presence and His miraculous provision. On our journey through life, when we are headed into new situations, we need to follow the ark, figuratively speaking, just as the Israelites followed the ark literally as they headed toward a new homeland. To "follow the ark" in our day is to follow the leading of the Holy Spirit, who lives within all believers.

The first question we need to ask when we face a new situation is, "Is this God's will for me?" The second is, "Do I have inner peace about this?" We also need to ask ourselves if we sense His presence in the new situation. If we believe it is God's will, we can trust God to provide everything we need each step of the way.

As a young woman, I didn't know how to seek God as I do now, and I made a decision I don't believe I would have made had I known how to follow the ark.

At eighteen years of age, I married the first young man who paid attention to me because I was afraid no one would ever want me, due to the sexual abuse I experienced as a child. I received Jesus as my Savior at the age of nine, but I never had any spiritual education or training after that point, so I'd never heard the idea of "being led by the Holy Spirit." I didn't know how to seek His guidance or realize that asking Him to lead me was important.

I look back now and see that the Holy Spirit was trying to lead me all along, because deep in my heart, I knew the relationship I was about to enter was not right. My mind told me I shouldn't miss this opportunity, but deep inside I felt uneasy about it. I simply didn't know what to do with the still, small voice telling me, "This will never work." But I was so desperate for someone to love me, I refused to pay attention to what I knew inside and I just followed my head, my flesh, my emotions, my plan, and my "want to."

The situation became five years of a terrible mess. This man and I often traveled to other states, and on two occasions—once in Oakland, California, and once in Albuquerque, New Mexico—he simply left me stranded and I had to leave all my meager possessions behind and return home on a bus. I was eighteen years old, lonely, frightened, and confused.

For most of the time we were married, he refused to work. He ran around with other women, lied, stole from me, and ended up going to prison for writing bad checks. One night I woke up and he was trying to remove my wedding ring from my finger so he could sell it. I could have saved myself five years of heartache and trouble had I simply known how to listen to God and allow Him to lead me into His perfect will for my life.

We need to "follow the ark" instead of following our personal desires, our fears, our emotions, our good ideas, or the advice of others. We follow the ark by taking one step of obedience to God after another.

The ark will lead us to new places, just as the Old Testament ark did the Israelites, because God does not take us backward. As we follow Him, we will find ourselves in unfamiliar places, uncomfortable places, or places in which we may be unsure of ourselves. Our journeys may not be easy, but personally, I would rather follow God into a new and uncomfortable place than remain in a place that is no longer life-giving for me.

> I would rather follow God into a new and uncomfortable place than remain in a place that is no longer life-giving for me.

FAILING TO FOLLOW

When we do God's will, His presence is with us and we are sure to succeed. But when we fail to follow Him, we invite all kinds of problems.

Some people have miserable lives for no other reason than the fact that they refuse to follow the leading of the Holy Spirit. Some people keep friends who influence them negatively. They may be fun to be with, or perhaps they've been friends for a long, long time, but they don't want to listen to God and obey His will. It's always best to have close friends who can build your faith in God rather than those who diminish it. Don't just decide who you'll be friends with, but ask God to give you relationships that are right for you.

Sometimes we pray for something but aren't willing to follow the Holy Spirit even when He tries to lead us into the answer to our prayer. For example, I know of people who refuse to attend singles groups at church because they don't want to go by themselves. Even when they believe God wants them to do so, they won't go. They want to date and eventually get married, but they want God to work on their terms. I can understand where it might take some courage to go alone, but doing the difficult thing is often good for us.

It stretches our faith and often leads us into the very thing we are looking for. We must be careful that we are not planning and praying that our plan will work, when we should be praying first and then following God's plan.

Are you willing to say yes to God even if it means saying no to your friends or even to yourself? What if you're invited to go somewhere with friends or a family member, but you don't have peace about going? It might be a party where people will be using drugs, or a movie that contains nudity. You'll have to compromise your conscience in order to go. What will you do? Are you willing to spend the evening at home alone in order to follow God?

In each of these situations, people who go ahead and do what they want to do are following their own desires over God's will. Is it possible, if they were to follow the leadership of the Holy Spirit, something truly wonderful would happen? Maybe a nice evening at home would provide the peace, quiet, rest, and refreshment they need after a hectic work week. Maybe they would make some new friends they could really enjoy if they would be bold enough to attend the singles group alone.

My daughter Sandra met her husband when she attended a church event all by herself. She was determined to follow God's leading, and she received a great blessing. I remember that it was difficult for her to go alone, but she told me that she was not going to sit home, get depressed, and complain about her life when she could make a different choice.

We need to be people who want to obey God and follow Him more than anything else. We need to be strong and courageous and do whatever God leads us to do. Even if you are the only person in the whole world doing the right thing, I encourage you to obey God. Do not follow your flesh, your friends, or your own wishes. Be like the Israelites who followed the ark and, by doing so, followed God into the good things He had for them.

YOU HAVE NOT PASSED THIS WAY BEFORE

I believe one of the most important verses in Joshua 3 is verse 4: "Yet a space must be kept between you and it, about 2,000 cubits by measure; come not near it, that you may [be able to see the ark and] know the way you must go, *for you have not passed this way before*" (emphasis mine).

These words grip my heart, and I want you to pay particular attention to them: "you have not passed this way before." Everything about those words says "new." Whether it is a job, a place to live, a relationship, an addition to your family, a position of influence, an exercise program, a church, a hobby, or a way of serving your community—if you have not passed that way before, it is new to you. You may not know how to get there or what to do when you do. But if you follow the ark (God), you will arrive at your destination and He will direct you in everything you need to do.

One of the biggest obstacles to following God is fear—simply because "you have not passed this way before." Things we have never done before always make us feel a little more timid than usual. People have asked me if I'm ever nervous or fearful, and my answer is yes. When I am doing something for the first time, or something I have no experience with, I am tempted to lose my confidence just like everyone else. My best advice is: press forward into what you believe God's will is for you. Don't let the feeling of fear rule your decisions. Be diligent to apply God's Word to your life and to stay close to Him.

When you follow God into a new place, you may feel stretched. Perhaps you receive a job promotion and you know you don't have all the natural skills and knowledge you need to do the new job well. Then you become worried or fearful because you think you're "in over your head." The job may be over your head, but it's not bigger than God. If He leads you into it, He will help you fulfill the responsibilities that go with it. God's power and presence enable us to do things we could not do on our own.

It's important to remember God is on your side as you go into new situations, because the enemy will always be lying in wait to try to keep you from following Him. Most of the time, he attempts to make us turn around and go back to our old circumstances by using the "what if" strategy. The goal of this scheme is to stir up such fear that you decide to not walk into the new place. In actuality, it looks something like this.

A man gets a new job in a new city. He and his wife have been praying for a new opportunity and a better job for him, and they believe this is it. They are so excited because God has orchestrated every aspect of the job search, the interview, and the offer. He has even blessed the man with a nice raise, and the new company is willing to pay moving expenses.

As the man prepares to write his resignation letter at his current job, a question enters his mind: *What if I end up having to work a lot more overtime than I have to work here?* He brushes that aside, but soon he wonders, *What if the cost of living is so much higher where we're going that my raise doesn't make much difference in our lifestyle?* Then he asks himself, *What if I don't even like the job after I've done it a while?*

That night, his wife says to him, "*I've been thinking: What if the children don't like their new school as much as they love their school here? What if we can't find a church as wonderful as our church here?*"

The man and his wife find themselves being tempted to walk away from the answer to their prayers, because of "what if" questions and lies. They have to stop relying on their minds and follow what God has placed in their hearts. They have to refuse to fear and begin thinking, *What if we are so radically happy in our new city we never want to come back here again? What if this job is the best thing to ever happen to our family?*

The enemy will call to your attention every possible "negative"

162   NEVER GIVE UP!

about a new situation, but he will not bother to mention any of
the positives. To focus on the positives, you have to spend time
with God and be willing to
follow the ark, as the Israelites did.

> *Don't be afraid to step out and do something new. Perhaps you haven't passed this way before, but God is with you.*

Don't be afraid to step out
and do something new. Perhaps you haven't passed
this way before, but God is
with you, so press through the fear and opposition, and refuse to
give up.

BE SENSITIVE TO GOD'S TIMING

Once you know something new is God's will for your life, you may
want to step into it before God releases you to do so. Or, after you
have had to wait for a while, you may decide you do not want to do
it after all! We should not run ahead of God or lag behind Him. God
has an appointed time for every purpose under heaven (see Ecclesi-
astes 3:1).

I tried to go on television before God opened the door for me,
and my project failed miserably. When His time came, I was thinking about settling into an easier schedule, and I didn't want to start
a major new endeavor. My plan at that time was to work less, not
more. Following God frequently means that we don't get to do things
our own way or according to our own timing.

Moses is a classic example of a man who struggled with God's
timing. God spared his life as a baby and then sent him to grow up
in Pharoah's palace. God had a great plan for Moses' life—a plan for
Moses to lead His people out of the bondage and slavery of Egypt
into freedom. But before God told Moses it was time to step out, he
took steps of his own. He saw an Egyptian mistreating one of his

kinsmen and, acting on his emotions, he killed the man. When he found out two Hebrew men witnessed the murder, he was afraid and he fled to the desert, where he stayed for forty years. The very fact that Moses behaved emotionally and fearfully shows he wasn't yet ready for the task God had in mind for him.

During his time in the desert, God worked with Moses, helped him grow up, and eventually revealed Himself to him in the burning bush (see Exodus 3:2). When God was ready to use him, Moses didn't want to cooperate. He asked God repeatedly to use someone else and gave Him all sorts of reasons he would not be a good deliverer. But Moses was God's choice, and after considerable protest, he did stand before Pharoah and speak on God's behalf. Like many of us, first he tried to step out too soon and then, when the time was right, he didn't want to step out at all.

I want you to know that God has His own timing. He may drop a dream, vision, or idea in your heart at one point in your life and then not ask you to do anything about it for years. In Moses' case, he underwent a forty-year training period in the desert before he was prepared to fulfill God's call on his life. I hope you do not have to wait that long, but if you do, just be patient. Resist the urge to get out in front of Him; and don't allow yourself to lag behind Him. Trying to move outside of His timing—either too quickly or too slowly—will cause you the kind of frustration that makes you want to give up, because His presence will not be there. Whether God asks you to wait two weeks or two decades, be sensitive to His timing in your life and be willing to wait for Him as He leads you into the next new place He has for you.

GOD WILL BE WITH YOU

In chapter 3, I made a brief reference to God's promise to Joshua: "As I was with Moses, so I will be with you" (Joshua 1:5). God repeats this pledge in Joshua 3:7: "This day I will begin to magnify you in the sight of all Israel, so they may know that *as I was with Moses, so I will be with you*" (emphasis mine).

God was calling Joshua into new territory. He was saying: "Come on now, Joshua, you've never done this before. You've never passed this way before. Previously, you worked under Moses. Moses carried all the main responsibility and you just helped him, but now Moses is gone. But you don't have to be concerned, and here's why: because as I was with Moses, so I will be with you."

I believe we allow ourselves to become overly concerned about our weaknesses. When faced with a new situation or opportunity, we often think of all the reasons why we can't do it: *I don't have enough experience. I don't have a college degree. I don't speak well in public. My computer skills are rusty. I don't know how to run a household. I'm not sure I will be a good parent. I've never been successful on a diet in my life. I just don't know if I will be able to do this new assignment.* This kind of self-doubt will sabotage you before you ever get to the new place God has for you. You will paralyze yourself with your own thinking. I call this "the paralysis of analysis."

The truth is, you don't have to be worried about your weaknesses. God is not at all surprised by them because He knows everything there is to know about you. God is not looking for *ability;* He's looking for *availability.* I encourage you to wake up every day and say: "Here I am, God. Is there anything You want me to do? Do You have something new for me? I'm going to be bold and courageous in You, Lord. If You want me to keep doing the same thing for another ten years, I can do it. And if You want me to launch out into something I have never done before, I can do that too because You are with me."

> *The truth is, you don't have to be worried about your weaknesses. God is not at all surprised by them.*

The Germinator

In Europe and the United States during the nineteenth century, many women died after giving birth in hospitals. Up to 25 percent of these new mothers contracted the aggressive infection puerperal sepsis, which was commonly called "childbed fever," and never recovered.

In the late 1840s, Dr. Ignaz Semmelweis, a young Hungarian doctor, worked in the maternity wards of a hospital in Vienna. The hospital had two maternity wards. Male medical students and physicians delivered babies in one, while female midwifery students attended the other. Semmelweis noticed that the rate of death from childbed fever was three to five times higher in the ward staffed by medical students than in the ward where midwives delivered babies.

At that time, no one understood the relationship between germs and disease, so the only way for Semmelweis to figure out why so many more women died at the hands of male physicians and medical students than under the care of midwives was to figure out what the two groups did differently. He soon realized the medical students often went straight from classes during which they performed autopsies and dissected corpses to attend women in labor.

Semmelweis acted on his hunch that the students might somehow be transferring disease from deceased patients to birthing mothers and ordered the men working in delivery rooms to wash their hands with a solution of chlorinated lime water before they examined the women. The results were astounding. With the hand-washing policy in place, the death rate in the ward dropped from more than 18 percent to less than 1.5 percent.

(continued)

We might think Semmelweis would be applauded for his outstanding work, but instead, he was widely and sharply criticized and even met with hostility. The director of the hospital where he worked felt Semmelweis had undermined his leadership, so he refused to grant the doctor any promotions or the teaching position he desired. His colleagues ridiculed him to the point that he eventually resigned and left his position at the hospital and returned to Hungary. In Hungary, Semmelweis took a job at a hospital where his methods reduced mortality rates from childbed fever to less than 1 percent.

Members of the medical community continued to dismiss Semmelweis's assertion that hand washing was a necessary step in reducing infection and death. In the midst of opposition, he held firm to his beliefs and wrote a book about them in the early 1860s. The scientific establishment ridiculed his book and continued to criticize his work.

In 1865, Semmelweis suffered a mental breakdown, which some attribute to the constant hostility and rejection he endured over his discovery of the importance of hand washing. His friends committed him to a mental institution where he died, ironically, of an infection of childbed fever, which he contracted through a cut finger.

We know today that Semmelweis was right. Science has proven the connection between germs and disease, and thorough hand-washing procedures are now mandatory in medical environments. Thankfully, Semmelweis never gave up on his scientific convictions and was willing to suffer for them so countless lives could be saved.

CHAPTER 12

YOUR OWN WORST ENEMY

*"Nothing is more wretched than the mind of
a man conscious of guilt."*
PLAUTUS

American poet and author Maya Angelou is known all over the world. I once read a biographical sketch on her and I want to share a portion of it with you:

> Maya Angelou was born Marguerite Annie Johnson in Saint Louis, Missouri. Her parents divorced when she was only three years old, and she and her brother, who gave her the nickname "Maya," were sent to live with their grandmother in the small town of Stamps, Arkansas. There, the young Maya endured racial discrimination, which was legal in America's southern states at that time. Also in Arkansas, she observed and absorbed powerful faith in God and the gentle manner and courtesy that marked the tradition of her African American people. Angelou says her grandmother and extended family taught her the values that later shaped her life and work.
>
> When Maya was seven years old, she went to visit her mother in Chicago, where she suffered sexual abuse by her

mother's boyfriend. The shame of that incident so paralyzed Angelou that she shared it with no one except her brother, with whom she had a close relationship. Later, she heard the news that her uncle had killed her attacker. The little girl believed, in some way, her words had murdered the man, and she did not speak for five years.

Can you imagine being a child and carrying such guilt you didn't speak for five years? Guilt is *that* powerful; it can silence a voice as eloquent and powerful as Angelou's. Feeling guilty is like being locked in an invisible prison cell. Guilt robs you of the ability to believe you are worthy of success in life, and you are never truly free as long as you carry its burden.

Jesus came to break the bondage of guilt in our lives. He paid with His life for everything we have ever done wrong and everything we will ever do wrong. When we believe in His work on the cross and receive Him as Lord and Savior, He looks at us and says, "Not guilty." We are justified in Christ Jesus, which means that God sees us as if we had never sinned. His sacrifice gave us the right to a brand-new life that includes success and enjoyment.

NO CONDEMNATION

"We all make mistakes." That phrase has been around for years, and it is certainly true. Equally true is the fact that most of us really *hate* making mistakes, doing things wrong, or causing problems. Many times, the guilt we feel over our mistakes is much worse than the mistakes themselves.

> *Many times, the guilt we feel over our mistakes is much worse than the mistakes themselves.*

We should of course be sorry when we do wrong, and we should always repent, which means to be willing to turn away from the sin and begin doing what is right with God's help. We may even need a brief time of grieving over very serious mistakes. But we are not supposed to hate ourselves, reject ourselves, and feel guilty and ashamed for days and weeks on end when we sin or make mistakes. We may feel *convicted* of sin when we do something wrong, but we should not experience condemnation. We are supposed to receive the forgiveness God freely offers us and go on with our lives, constantly seeking to know God better and better.

The apostle Paul had plenty of reasons to feel guilty. He'd persecuted and killed many Christians before he had a personal encounter with Jesus Christ and began to follow Him. In Romans 8:1, this man who knew what it means to be both guilty and free of guilt writes: "Therefore, [there is] now no condemnation (no adjudging guilty of wrong) for those who are in Christ Jesus, who live [and] walk not after the dictates of the flesh, but after the dictates of the Spirit."

Human nature causes us to feel condemned when we make mistakes, and no one likes feelings of condemnation. Many people I know want to do everything right, but that isn't going to happen as long as we're in bodies of flesh. If we could be perfect in our behavior, we wouldn't need God and we would miss out on the enjoyment and blessings of a relationship with Him. Jesus died for us because we could not be good enough on our own to enjoy a relationship with God who is completely holy.

Sometimes, because we feel guilty over our sins or mistakes, we struggle to enjoy God or the lives He has given us. No matter how hard we try, we will never be able to live without making mistakes. If we believe we have to suffer and feel terrible and go on a guilt trip every time we make a mistake, then our lives will be miserable. The way to overcome this is by faith.

We must believe the truth of God's Word more than we believe our emotions or our

> *No matter how hard we try, we will never be able to live without making mistakes.*

thoughts. It really is possible to *know* in the depths of our hearts that we are not guilty, even if we *feel* we are. At such times, we need to confess the truth of God's Word instead of focusing on our feelings.

If you want to honor God, put your faith to work believing God forgives you immediately when you ask Him to do so. Even if you *feel* guilty you can be assured you are not because 1 John 1:9 says: "If we [freely] admit that we have sinned and confess our sins, He is faithful and just (true to His own nature and promises) and will forgive our sins [dismiss our lawlessness] and [continuously] cleanse us from all unrighteousness [everything not in conformity to His will in purpose, thought, and action]." When feelings of guilt and condemnation arise, press through them in faith and say, "I don't care how I feel. I have been forgiven!" People will never enjoy God's plan for their lives unless they stop making decisions based on feelings. Honor God by deciding to trust His Word more than you trust your feelings.

PAID IN FULL

Reportedly, the IRS once received a letter that read:

"Dear IRS, I have cheated on my taxes many, many times. I can't remember ever paying what I owed. I feel so guilty about this that I cannot sleep at night. Please find enclosed a check for $20,000.00. P.S.: If I still have trouble sleeping, I'll send more money."

Guilt will cause people to do unusual things. Most of the time, guilt is nothing more than our pathetic way of sacrificing something to make up for what we've done wrong. The truth is, either Jesus did a complete and thorough job when He paid for our sins at the cross and does not need our help, or He did not finish the work. I assure you, He finished the work; He was the final, the only, the complete sacrifice ever needed for our sin. No additional sacrifice will ever need to be made. In my case, I finally realized that I was punishing myself with feelings of guilt and refusing to do anything I might enjoy as a way of paying for my imperfections. I also realized that my pathetic attempt was not pleasing, nor was it acceptable to God at all.

We humans tend to divide our sins into categories. We determine how big or bad we think a certain sin is and then decide how long we should feel rotten about it in order to pay for it. We also feel we have no right to be blessed, succeed at anything, or enjoy ourselves until we satisfy the debt.

You may be thinking, *Now wait a minute, Joyce, I can't just do something wrong and not care about it.* I have even thought that myself in the past. Let me say this: if you are a true believer in Jesus Christ, there is no way you could ever sin and not care. That is not possible because He has given you a new heart. You know sin offends God, and you love God, so of course you will care. But there is a difference between caring about your sin and feeling condemned because of it. Caring about it simply means the convicting power of the Holy Spirit is at work in a heart that is tender toward God, but feeling guilty and condemned is an indication that the enemy is at work. Always remember to receive conviction, which is from the Holy Spirit, but aggressively reject condemnation, which is from the enemy.

THE GUILT CYCLE

Many years ago, I was on the evangelism board at a church Dave and I attended. Every Wednesday night, we walked around neighborhoods, knocking on doors and telling people about Jesus.

At that time, I really loved God, but I was "doing" witnessing, not *being* a witness. I didn't understand that Jesus promised that the Holy Spirit would give us power to *be* His witnesses, not simply to do the activity of witnessing (see Acts 1:8). In order to *be* a witness, I had to let God teach me the truth of His Word and change my heart and behavior. I was controlling, manipulative, selfish, and angry. I was frustrated, aggravated, upset, and generally hard to get along with.

Over time, I did receive the power to "be." That doesn't mean I never make mistakes or never have a bad day, but it does mean I have more good days than bad ones. My behavior has improved dramatically since those days and continues to get better and better all the time.

I want you to understand that my improvement was very difficult and extremely slow for a long time. I didn't make much significant progress until I learned how to break the cycle of guilt in my life. If I made a mistake on Monday, I spent Tuesday, Wednesday, and part of Thursday feeling guilty about what happened on Monday. So I ruined not only Monday for myself but also Tuesday, Wednesday, and Thursday. By the time Thursday afternoon rolled around, I finally felt a little better because I believed I had suffered long enough to pay for what I did on Monday.

> *I didn't make much significant progress until I learned how to break the cycle of guilt in my life.*

Then what do you think happened on Thursday afternoon, just as I was finally starting to feel good about myself again? I made another mistake on Thursday night. Then Thursday night was ruined, which led to my feeling bad on Friday, Saturday, and Sunday. In the course of an entire week, I had only a few hours of freedom from guilt. What a miserable existence!

We must realize guilt does not change us, but it does trap us in the cycle of sin and more guilt. The truth is, the guilt itself is sin because the Bible says whatever is not of faith is sin. Guilt is certainly not something we have by faith, because it is rooted in fear. A right response to sin is to receive conviction from God, admit the sin, confess it, turn from it, and receive God's complete forgiveness through Jesus Christ.

I have learned to receive forgiveness quickly, because I know God wants me to have a joyful, blessed life. He wants the same for you. Guilt will steal your joy and blessings, but you can enjoy life and have the strength to keep going if you learn to repent *quickly,* receive forgiveness *quickly,* and *quickly* get back to doing what you are supposed to do instead of staying trapped in guilt and condemnation.

> *You can enjoy life and have the strength to keep going if you learn to repent* quickly, *receive forgiveness* quickly, *and* quickly *get back to doing what you are supposed to do.*

DOUBLE PAYMENT

In Philippians 3:8–12, Paul is basically saying he wanted to be perfect, but had not yet attained it; he knew he had not yet "arrived." Read his words in verses 13–14: "I do not consider, brethren, that I have captured and made it my own [yet]; *but one thing I do* [it is my one aspiration]: forgetting what lies behind and straining forward to what lies ahead, I press on toward the goal to win the [supreme and heavenly] prize to which God in Christ Jesus is calling us upward" (emphasis mine).

Notice Paul writes: "but one thing I do." What was his "one thing," the thing he knew would help him make more progress than anything else he could do? It was forgetting what was behind him. How do we forget what lies behind us, the situations in our pasts, especially those things that cause us to feel guilty? We simply stop thinking about them and stop talking about them, and we press on to the good things ahead.

Many times when we teach on Philippians 3, we stop with verse 14, but I want you to see something powerful in verses 15–16: "So let those [of us] who are spiritually mature and full-grown have this mind and hold these convictions; and if in any respect you have a different attitude of mind, God will make that clear to you also. Only let us hold true to what we have already attained and walk and order our lives by that."

Paul is saying people who are spiritually mature know how to let go of past mistakes and go on without suffering for days on end. He is indicating that people who feel guilty and bad about themselves every time they make mistakes still need to grow up in God because they are spiritually immature.

Spiritual maturity says, "I have a job to do. God's called me; He's gifted me; He's put me in this place; I have an assignment. I don't have time to be trapped in guilt over what I did wrong last week; I need to live today! I want to change and grow spiritually, but I know I must let go of past mistakes. Jesus' sacrifice gives me the right to succeed."

We must come to the point in life where we decide whether we really believe what the Bible says or not. Do we believe Jesus took our sins upon Himself and that He took our punishment, rose from the dead, and is interceding for us before the Father right now? Do we believe Jesus is our substitute and that what He did for us we do not have to do again? If we do believe He did these things for us, then we need to act on that belief and refuse to stay trapped in yesterday's mistakes. He always calls us to go forward, so we need to forget what lies behind us and go on.

I remember well when God taught me this lesson in a profound way. I was a committed Christian; I already had a ministry; and I was teaching a Bible study. But I felt guilty almost all the time. I always had a vague feeling on the inside that something simply was not right about me. Over and over again in my mind, I wondered, *What's wrong with me?*

One day I went shopping and parked my car in the back of the store's parking lot. I still chuckle when I think of that because it certainly was not the kind of car anyone would want to steal. Maybe I parked in the back of the lot because I felt so pitiful, as though I didn't deserve to park closer to the store.

I had done something wrong that day, and as I was walking into the store, the Lord posed a question in my heart, asking me how I was going to deal with my sin.

I responded, "Oh, I'll just receive the sacrifice Jesus made when He died on Calvary."

God then continued to place different things in my heart: *I see, and when do you plan to do that?*

I suddenly understood what He was trying to show me, and said, "Oh, probably in about three days."

He continued: *Don't you realize all you are doing is trying to pay for your sin and I have already done that? You can't pay for your sin. I've done it through the sacrifice of My Son.*

The Lord then impressed upon me that I would be doing Him a favor to receive His forgiveness and simply let go of the guilt and get on with His business. He showed me He was trying to use me and I was of no value to Him in the negative, downtrodden position I was in.

None of us can be of value to God while we're trapped in guilt and condemning feelings. Only immature Christians beat themselves up for every mistake they make. But mature believers apply the work of the cross in their lives, accepting by faith that Jesus shed His blood to forgive our sins, receiving His forgiveness, and going on about the things God has called us to do without a trace of guilt. This may be a new way of thinking for you, but it is biblical and it is your right as a believer in Jesus Christ.

THE RIGHT TO FEEL GOOD

You have a blood-purchased right to feel good about yourself and to succeed in life without feeling guilty. I want you to think about this: Jesus paid for your freedom with His own blood. He purchased you and set you free from slavery to sin and guilt. *You have a right to feel good about yourself and to succeed in life without feeling guilty.* You do not even have to be in the neutral zone and feel "okay" about yourself; you can actually feel good. Not only have you been set free from feeling bad about yourself, you can like yourself!

Dave is a very happy, peaceful person. For years, people have asked him, "What's it like for you for Joyce to be the one in front of people? Doesn't that bother you?"

Dave did go through some transition in the early years, but it didn't take him long at all to accept completely that I was called to be more visible than he is. He is the type of person who simply sets his mind to agree with God.

When our ministry first began to take on a public component, Dave complained to God, saying, "Well, this doesn't seem fair. The man is usually the one who is most visible and 'out front.' Why haven't You anointed me to teach, God?"

Dave knew God does not have to explain Himself or justify His actions to anyone. I'm not sure exactly how He answered Dave's question, but I do know Dave soon came to me and said, "It's obvious that God has anointed you to do what you're doing. It's obvious He has called you and I believe He wants me to back you up and be your covering. I just want to tell you, from now on I'm with you; I'm for you. I'll go where you go."

One of the main reasons Dave is such a happy, contented person is that he never walks around feeling belittled because I often receive more public attention than he does. He does not feel guilty about what he is not called or anointed to do. He knows what he is anointed to do; he is great at those things; and he enjoys doing them. He is never in competition with me. He is happy because he knows who he is and he likes himself.

Many people are not like Dave, though. They don't like themselves and they don't feel secure in who they are. In fact, I used to be that way. But now, I have a good relationship with myself. I like the person God created when He made me.

I'll never forget being in a certain city and seeing the newspaper headline that read: "Meyer says she likes herself!" I am not sure why that was newsworthy, but perhaps it was because society views having a low self-image as admirable and has somehow convinced us we are arrogant if we actually like ourselves. I believe something is wrong with that mentality. Self-hatred is often connected with being religious; and it leads to all kinds of bondage. God loves us, so we need to love ourselves, not in a haughty way, but in a healthy, balanced, biblical way because we believe He who knew no sin became sin for us so we might be made the righteousness of God in Christ (see 2 Corinthians 5:21). We have no right to hate what God purchased with the blood of His Son, our Lord and Savior, Jesus Christ. God loves us and we need to agree with Him, not with the devil who tries to make us feel guilty.

Small Change, Big Changes

Some of the greatest blessings of my life have resulted from opportunities to be a blessing to someone else. One of the most powerful stories I know is the remarkable account of Osceola McCarty, a woman who refused to give up on her dream of helping others receive a benefit she never had.

The Mississippi native was born in 1908 to a mother who had to work long, hard hours to raise young Osceola alone. She worked as a cook for a local county clerk and sold candy at the local school to make extra money. Surrounded by need and influenced by her mother's work ethic, Osceola began working at a young age and saved the money she earned by ironing after school.

Osceola had already decided she wanted money to help care for her grandmother in her old age, and when she was in the sixth grade, she also realized one of her aunts needed her help. That aunt had no children, so when she was unable to walk after a hospital stay, Osceola had to help her. By the time her aunt had improved enough for Osceola to return to school, her fellow students had advanced so far beyond her she decided to not go back.

So the kindhearted young girl began a career that would last decades. She simply did what she knew how to do—washing and ironing. And she did it for years. Osceola charged $1.50 to $2.00 per bushel to do laundry in the early days. As the cost of living increased, so did her prices. When she reached the point where she had to charge $10.00 per bushel, the frugal washwoman became more committed than ever to saving money. She put it in her existing savings account, and more remarkably, she refused to take it out. She just left it—and it grew.

As her savings became significant, her bankers encouraged

her to let her money work for her, suggesting ways it would earn more interest than it did in savings accounts. She took their advice, and her balances continued to increase. Even though Osceola, who never married, had money in the bank, she kept washing and ironing. She lived conservatively; she did not have a car; her house was not air-conditioned for many years; and she walked everywhere she went, even pushing her own shopping cart about a mile to buy groceries.

Osceola's hometown of Hattiesburg, Mississippi, is also home to one of the state's universities—the University of Southern Mississippi. At one point during Osceola's lifetime, the school did not admit black students. By the time she was older, they did—the woman with only a sixth-grade education wanted to use her money to give deserving African American students in financial need the opportunity to receive a college degree. So, in 1995, she donated $150,000 to the university and established the Osceola McCarty Scholarship. In an interview after her gift became public knowledge, McCarty said: "I can't do everything, but I can do something to help somebody. And what I can do, I will do."

Let me encourage you to think of ways you can bless others, as Osceola McCarty did. Have some kind of dream that involves more than getting ahead personally, but that also includes helping people. Be as committed to that dream as you are to other goals you set in life.

CHAPTER 13

NEVER BE ASHAMED

"True innocence never feels shame."
JEAN-JACQUES ROUSSEAU

You may know the story of a quiet, courageous woman named Rosa Parks, a hardworking African American seamstress who refused to surrender her bus seat to a white man. At that time, in the mid-1950s, the law required African Americans to give their seats to white people, to use separate restrooms and water fountains, and to submit themselves to all sorts of shameful rules and regulations for no other reason than the fact they were not white. These people suffered terribly because of who they were, not because of anything they did.

Rosa Parks pressed past the shame society put on her because of her race when she kept her seat that December day in 1955. Upon her death in 2005, she was the first woman to lie in state at the United States Capitol. Imagine that! A woman who was once refused a seat on a bus because of who she was decided one day to throw off the cloak of shame she had worn all her life. Her refusal to submit to shame launched a movement that rolled the reproach off an entire race of people, and her courage earned her a place of honor in American history.

IT'S ABOUT WHO YOU ARE

You cannot press through the challenges and difficulties of life if down deep inside of you, in the core of your being, you are ashamed of who you are. I'm not talking about being embarrassed because of something you've done, but about *who you are*. Guilt is a feeling you have about what you do; shame relates to who you are as a person. Shame and guilt are very close relatives, but shame lodges far deeper in a person's heart than guilt does, and I believe it is a more serious issue.

Shame often hides in your very nature, in the depth of your soul. It manifests itself as a constant feeling of uneasiness, a low-level but continual sense of condemnation, and a never-ending internal whisper that tells you, "You're not good enough." It is evident in the way you feel about yourself, relate to others, view relationships, and think about opportunities that present themselves to you.

YOU'RE NOT WHO YOU WERE

A person who is abused almost always develops a shame-based nature. That was certainly true for me. The sexual abuse I suffered as a child produced a root of shame deep inside of me. Early on, I was simply ashamed of what my father was doing to me, but at some point during my childhood, I stopped being ashamed of what he was doing and became terribly ashamed of myself because he was doing it to me. I thought, *Something must be wrong with me if he wants to do this to me.* I now understand that by thinking that way, I poisoned my soul. Everything in me became tainted as the destructive power of shame coursed through my thoughts and personality. I took on a false sense of responsibility; I took on myself the blame and shame for someone else's sin.

Now that shame is gone. I have been set free through God's love and acceptance. I am able to say, "I was abused as a child; I was filled with hatred and bitterness; I was unwilling to forgive my father for abusing me; I was ashamed of who I was; I became a very unpleasant person who tried to control everything and everyone." I can tell you all about what I was because the events that caused such shame are in the past and the characteristics I previously displayed do not describe me anymore. When Jesus died on the cross, I died with Him; when He was raised to a new life, I was raised with Him. I am a new creature in Christ; old things have passed away and all things are made brand new (see 2 Corinthians 5:17). The same thing is true for you if you have accepted Jesus as your Savior.

Whatever is in your past, do not feel ashamed and as if you must hide it. Telling everyone you know for no reason might not be wise, but if you do need to tell someone, don't be ashamed to do it. What God has delivered you from may encourage other people to believe they can receive help too.

When I think about the terrible situations I encountered as a child—some of the things I endured—and especially when I have a reason to talk about them, I honestly feel I am talking about someone I knew long ago, not myself. Freedom is not letting your yesterday affect your today. What you were is not what you are! You are God's child now, and your future is bright.

> *Freedom is not letting your yesterday affect your today.*

CHARACTERISTICS OF A SHAME-BASED NATURE

I believe, more than anything, that all of us simply want to be free to be who we are and to be accepted for who we are—and shame keeps us from being able to do that. The word *shame* means "to be confounded, confused, dry, disappointed, and stopped." To be confounded means "to be defeated, overthrown, and damned." The word *damned* means "doomed to punishment." Therefore, if we have shame-based natures, we are doomed to punishment. We punish ourselves every day by hating ourselves, rejecting ourselves, and being ashamed and embarrassed because of who we are. People in this condition have no idea how wonderful life could be if they would simply stop being ashamed and learn to accept themselves.

People with shame-based natures may exhibit a variety of personality traits or struggle with a number of issues because of the shame and sense of unworthiness in their lives. I want to call some of these issues to your attention so you can overcome them or help someone else break free from shame and live in the wonderful acceptance Jesus died to give us.

Depression

People who have shame-based natures often are depressed. They're emotionally down, discouraged, and hopeless because they feel terrible about themselves. Many people battling depression alienate themselves from others. They live isolated lives full of self-doubt and totally lacking in confidence. If you've had a lifetime struggle with depression, ask yourself, *How do I feel about myself?* No medicine can change the way you feel about yourself. I encourage you to see a doctor if you need to, but more importantly you should saturate yourself with the truth of God's Word and begin to renew your mind on who He says you are, because that will change the way you feel about yourself.

I know many people struggle with anxiety, depression, and other conditions that significantly reduce their ability to enjoy life. With God's help, I have overcome many of these issues, but I have experienced few "instant breakthroughs" on the road to healing. Most of the time, leaving these problems behind has to be done one step at a time.

Perfectionism

Perfectionists receive their self-worth by trying to do everything right so people will applaud them and tell them how perfect they are. Some become addicted to approval from others. Do you know how painful it is to be addicted to approval and the kind of person who becomes angry or unhappy if others offer healthy constructive criticism, correction, or even suggestions? You have to get to the point where somebody can say, "I don't like your hair that way," and you can say, "You know what? I do." Or someone might say, "I don't think that color looks good on you." But you can say, "Okay, but I love it." This does not mean you should be belligerent and never take advice from anybody. Please keep the balance. I'm simply saying that if you are addicted to others' approval, you will never have any freedom. Satan can arrange ten times every day to find somebody who gives you the wrong look, the wrong glance, or the wrong word that will cause you to try to change yourself to suit others; so, therefore, you are never true to yourself.

Because of the abuse I endured as a child and the root of shame it produced, I suffered horrible guilt every time I failed to perform perfectly. That intense guilt and shame rendered me unable to do much that would make a difference or amount to anything for God. It was an underlying pressure that drained me of the ability to enjoy anything I did.

Hard-Heartedness

People who struggle with toxic, poisonous shame are often cold and unfriendly. I was like that—extremely hard-hearted, cold, and unfriendly. I thought I didn't need anyone. I refused to allow anyone to really get close to me because I imagined they wouldn't like me if they really knew me. I was afraid to open my heart to anyone because I thought they would hurt me. So I managed to keep them out. People living with this kind of shame are often quick-tempered. Deep down inside they're angry about their lives and the things that have happened to them, but they express it wrongly. Hard-hearted people usually have an edge of harshness about them and spend their lives being misunderstood. Everyone thinks they are mean, but in reality they're deeply wounded and hurt. Always remember, "hurting people hurt people."

Fear

Shame-based nature produces timidity and fear of all types, and compulsive issues such as: eating disorders, gambling, drugs, alcohol, excessive spending, stealing, lying, and sexual perversions. People who suffer these things may become workaholics. Or they often hide by spending excessive time on the computer or watching television. They can even hide from themselves by sleeping too much. They say they are just tired, but the truth is they are probably tired of themselves.

False or Excessive Responsibility

I never really knew what neurosis was until I studied it—and then I realized it was a big problem for me. People who are neurotic take on too much responsibility, and in conflict they always assume they are at fault.

For many years, I had a false sense of responsibility. I didn't know that was what was wrong with me, but I felt so pressured—so burdened—under the weight of everything I thought people expected me to do and all of my so-called assignments in life. The only problem was: I had assigned them to myself! No one had put those burdens on myself but me.

Once again, this issue was rooted in my childhood. While I was being abused by my father, I was trying to keep it from my mother. My mother was a sweet lady who got hurt all the time; I didn't want her to hurt anymore. I was afraid of my father. He said to me repeatedly, "You'd better not tell." Under those circumstances, I constantly tried to keep everyone "fixed." I didn't want to make Daddy angry, and I didn't want Daddy to become upset with Mom because I knew his anger would cause him to mistreat her. So I had to keep Daddy happy; I had to keep Mother happy. I had one brother, and I tried to keep him from finding out or getting hurt. I thought I had to keep everything fixed. So in an almost unconscious way, I became the peacemaker in the house. The minute anything went wrong, I tried to fix it. I spent my life thinking, *Uh-oh, Dad's getting mad. What can I do to bring peace?* This habit led to a false sense of responsibility that I dealt with for years and years and still have to guard against.

Being responsible is a good quality, but taken too far, even a good thing can become a problem. Do you tend to feel responsible for everything that doesn't work out right? If you have a child who didn't turn out as you hoped, do you think it's your fault? Neurotic people always assume situations and circumstances are their fault. You may be wondering, *What could I have done differently so my child would have turned out better?* You know what? Sometimes you can do everything right, and people still make wrong choices in their lives. We must stop taking the responsibility for everything that goes on in the world, and begin to live our own lives and enjoy them. Don't let someone else's bad choice affect your joy.

NAKED AND UNASHAMED

The Bible says that Adam and Eve were in the garden with no sin; they were naked and unashamed. I believe this lets us know that God wants us to be completely open and honest, first with ourselves and then with others. If we want to live victorious Christian lives, we have to accept the fact that Jesus took our shame on the cross.

There is far too much pretense in the world. People try really hard to cover up their weaknesses, mistakes, and sins. Even though many people hide behind much pretense, they're actually longing to see someone who is genuine and real. As Christians we should be willing to set examples for the world to follow.

In Genesis 3:7, 21 we see Adam and Eve tried to cover themselves after they sinned. Similarly, we try to cover up all kinds of things about ourselves. How do we do this? We make excuses; we blame other people; we pretend things do not bother us when they do.

My daughter Sandra had frequent outbreaks of pimples as a teenager. She put so much makeup on those pimples trying to cover them up that she actually drew attention to them. Similarly, I tried so hard to cover up the abuse in my childhood that I ended up with a rough, tough "I don't need anybody" attitude that actually drew attention to me. People knew something was not right. They didn't know what it was, but I do recall being asked, "What is wrong with you?"

The truth is I was hurting and lonely and afraid, but I didn't know how to tell anyone, so I tried to cover it with a pretend personality I thought would keep others from getting too close to me.

Many people do not know who they are. They have tried to be so many people, they lost themselves long ago. If this describes you, I encourage you to stop trying to be like somebody else. Stop trying to put on an act for others and just be real. You do not need to cover yourself or hide behind anything or anybody. Be brave enough to put your shame aside and let the real you step into the light for the people around you to see and enjoy. Start by being really open with God. Tell Him everything about yourself—your secret thoughts, fears, and desires. He already knows everything before you tell Him, but doing so will be a type of release as you begin being totally honest with someone you can trust, and God is that someone. He knows all about you and loves you unconditionally. The more you are open with yourself and God, the more you will be able to be genuine with other people.

> *The more you are open with yourself and God, the more you will be able to be genuine with other people.*

LET ME INTRODUCE YOU

You are a wonderful person, and if you have suffered under the weight of shame for most of your life, allow me to reintroduce you to yourself. You need to meet the *real* you because you have been deceived into thinking you are someone you are not. You might say you have been the victim of identity theft. You are a child of God. His power is in you and He will enable you to do whatever you need to do in life. You are a new creation, the righteousness of God in Christ (see 2 Corinthians 5:17,21). You have an assignment from God and a great future. Your past has been washed away in the blood of Jesus. You are awesome—totally, absolutely awesome! The Bible says many wonderful things about you, and you need to learn what they are by reading and studying it. Don't ever allow what someone else thinks or says about you to be the factor that determines your value, because what God says is the only things that really matters.

Psalm 34:4–5 says, "I sought (inquired of) the Lord and required Him [of necessity and on the authority of His Word], and He heard me, and delivered me from all my fears. They looked to Him and were radiant; their faces shall never blush for shame or be confused."

Let me urge you today to seek the Lord, require Him in your daily life, and trust the authority of His Word. Look to Him, and He will set you free from shame. As you press past the shame you have carried in your life, you will be able to be and do everything God has called you to be and do. Embrace the unconditional acceptance God offers you through Jesus Christ and you will have the power to never give up.

From Darkness Into the Light

During the fall of Michelle's sophomore year in college, her life became overwhelming to her—even though nothing identifiable was wrong with her. In addition to anxiety, she struggled with everyday activities, she suffered a dramatic loss of energy, and her sense of hope for the future—and the present—took a major nosedive. Without intervention, Michelle's hope, energy, and coping abilities began to return as spring approached. By April of that year, she was her old self again.

Little did she know that depression would become the norm for her for months at a time over the course of the next twenty years. At first she thought she simply struggled adjusting to school each fall, but even after she finished college and began her career, every autumn as the leaves fell to the ground, her moods and outlook on life plummeted too. Her symptoms grew worse with every passing year—to the point that she often wanted to die and be with the Lord and thought she had done so when she awoke in the middle of the night.

Michelle sought all kinds of help—counseling (both psychological and pastoral), doctors, nutritionists—but no one could help her. She eventually enrolled in a clinical trial at the National Institutes of Mental Health in Bethesda, Maryland, and became one of the first people in the world to be diagnosed with seasonal affective disorder.

Thrilled to have a diagnosis, but deeply upset by the knowledge of that ongoing chemical glitch in her brain chemistry, she returned to her home and career in New York and tried to hold on to her life. For the next seven years, she and her doctor worked to find the right balance of extending her day artificially by sitting

(continued)

for four hours a day under a very bright full spectrum light and taking antidepressant medication, which was extremely difficult for her to choose to do. Her Christian training and upbringing had taught her that her daily walk with God would give her strength, and that God could heal her depressions.

Today, Michelle knows the Lord saved her life. "I was so frustrated for so many years," she says. "I couldn't understand why God wouldn't give me relief...it seemed so little to ask. But God's ways aren't our ways, and His timing is often different than ours would be. But He does give us the strength to go through our afflictions and the insight to be able to use our suffering in constructive ways. Now I know that although God didn't heal me, He did save my life. Without His grace, I can say without hesitation that I wouldn't be here today."

CHAPTER 14

YOUR SECRET WEAPON

"How much more grievous are the consequences of anger than the causes of it."

MARCUS AURELIUS

Vincent Newfield worked at our ministry, and I want you to read this story that he shared with us:

> Has God ever spoken something very strong in your heart? He did to me in November 1998. While sitting in my closet praying, the Lord spoke to my heart and said, I am moving you and your family to St. Louis to work for Joyce Meyer. Your gift will be a blessing to her, and you and your family will be blessed greatly.
>
> *Wow! Was that really God? He had never spoken to me that way before.* Repeatedly, His words rang in my ears for weeks. The strange thing was, I had yet to fill out an application or send in my resume. But in January 1999, I did. Within weeks my references were being called. I was in awe. *Could God have really spoken to me? I thought.* Is He really moving us to St. Louis? *A new journey of faith began to unfold.*
>
> *March came and I was contacted by the ministry. After two interviews by phone, I was sent a sample writing assignment. After sweating it out for three weeks, I received*

word that they liked it. The next step would be a face-to-face interview in June. I couldn't believe it! What God had said in my heart was actually happening, and rather quickly. Excitement, hope, and joy filled my soul. My faith had risen to an all-time high. Then . . . the bottom dropped out.

On May 12, 1999, I received one of the most discouraging phone calls of my life. "Vincent, I am sorry to inform you that the interview has been cancelled. The writing position you applied for has been put on hold for six months to a year." My heart sank within me. All hope, happiness, and faith were gone. What happened? I don't understand. Things were moving along, and then suddenly it's over. *Allison, my wife, stood faithfully beside me, encouraging me to not give up hope. "If God spoke to you, it's going to happen," she said. "It's just a matter of time."*

After three days I mustered enough faith to listen to a teaching tape by Charles Stanley fittingly titled Unshakable Faith. *Slowly but surely, God encouraged me as I drove and listened. A ray of hope began breaking forth on the horizon of my heart. Then all of a sudden, WHAM! I found myself in one of the worst accidents ever. My car was totaled, and I was further humiliated to find that the accident was my fault. Feeling totally discouraged, I returned home and discovered that both of our computers broke earlier that day. We published a magazine and this meant it couldn't be finished. Its theme, ironically, was "Encouragement in the Face of Hopelessness."*

Seething anger was now surging. "Where are You, God? What are You doing? I don't understand? Why are You allowing this in my life?" For days on end, disappointment, discouragement, and despair became very close friends. Question after question filled my mind. The biggest one that would haunt me was: Did I really hear from God about moving to St. Louis? *I tried with everything in me to forget about St. Louis and working for Joyce Meyer, but it* never *went away. It seemed like everywhere I looked, I saw St. Louis, Missouri—license plates, garbage can lids, household cleaners, you name it.*

God made a way for us to finish that issue of the magazine and taught me a tremendous lesson in patience, endurance, and trusting Him. My faith had been put to the test. Each day I had a choice to believe God had spoken to my heart or reject it. I cried many tears and experienced a wide range of emotions, including anger and depression. But deep inside, I wanted to believe, and my willingness to trust in God's track record kept me going.

Over a year had passed; it was now July 2000. Allison and I had published the last issue of our magazine, and I was looking for new employment. One more time, I thought. I'll send Joyce Meyer Ministries some updated sample work and call them one more time. That was nearly seven years ago. Since then I have been given the awesome privilege of writing for Dave and Joyce and overseeing her monthly magazine, which impacts millions every month.

My point: If God has put something in your heart that will not seem to go away, keep on believing. He will bring it to pass. Cry if you have to... work through anger, frustration, and doubt... but don't give up.

PUSH THROUGH ANGER AND UNFORGIVENESS

Vincent admitted that he was angry at times during the long process of making the changes he wanted. Everyone is tempted to be angry occasionally; we may even be tempted to stay angry for days, weeks, or months on end. The Bible acknowledges that we will be angry at times, but it clearly instructs us not to stay angry. We need to be people who are "calm, cool, and collected" because we have learned how to handle our anger and disappointment in a biblical way. Scripture plainly tells us: "When angry, do not sin; do not ever let your wrath (your exasperation, your fury or indignation) last until the sun goes down" (Ephesians 4:26). We can *be* angry, but we must not *stay* angry; we can be disappointed, but we need to get reappointed. God will always give us a new beginning when something did not work out the way we planned. We need to learn to keep our hearts completely cleansed of all negative emotions because they war against our peace.

If we don't deal with our negative emotions, we will soon find ourselves with all kinds of problems, including physical ones. For example, if we are angry with someone and stay angry long enough to let that anger take root in our hearts, we will develop a root of bitterness (see Hebrews 12:15) and become resentful and miserable. The longer we allow ourselves to remain that way, the more negatively it affects our health. Try to remember that being upset takes a lot of energy and unless you have energy to waste I suggest you learn how to stay calm, cool, and collected.

I am continually amazed by the number of people I encounter who love God and are trying to move forward with Him while still harboring anger, unforgiveness, or other negative emotions in their hearts. Sometimes they are angry at someone for a situation or offense that happened many years ago. They often say, "Well, I have really tried to get over this, but I just can't." Yes, they can. God does not ever ask us to do anything impossible. If He tells us to forgive, then we can forgive. If He tells us not to be offended, then there is a way for us to keep from being offended. He tells us to stay calm, cool, and collected; therefore, it is possible to do it.

> *God does not ever ask us to do anything impossible. If He tells us to forgive, then we can forgive.*

WHAT'S THAT SMELL?

Many times, where anger and other negative emotions are concerned, we stuff them deep in our hearts and pretend nothing is wrong. Negative emotions buried alive never die; they have to be thoroughly dealt with or they will keep showing up one way or another. Anger and unforgiveness, for example, have roots, deep underlying feelings that result in angry outbursts and unkind actions. They can even be the root cause of depression. We may develop ways of ignoring our negative feelings and finding temporary relief, but rotten roots always produce rotten fruit; and before long, that root of anger will produce more ugly feelings and behaviors, which may be a little different from our previous feelings, but still come from the same root.

I'm sure you have experienced opening your refrigerator door and noticing a bad odor. Immediately you wonder, *What's that horrible smell?* The only way to eliminate the smell is to find its source. You may cover it up temporarily with some kind of deodorizer, but unless it's completely eliminated, it always comes back.

Most of the time, the odor doesn't come from something in the front of the refrigerator. It is usually something hidden, something you would not even think could cause such a stink. You have to take everything out of the refrigerator, piece by piece, to discover the source of the smell. You have to clear the shelves and go through the drawers until, at last, you finally find an old, moldy, unidentifiable piece of food you had long forgotten!

I've run across many people who say their lives are like their refrigerators—they stink. When this happens, they have to examine every aspect of their hearts to find the cause of the problem. Often, the source is anger or offense they have denied, covered, or tried to hide. It lurks in the hidden places of the heart, causing great damage and breeding rottenness in the core of a person. Just as a little puff of deodorizer will not cover a terrible smell in a refrigerator, trying to camouflage deeply rooted anger and unforgiveness or other negative emotions will not eliminate the cause of the bad attitudes and actions that result.

We must stop trying to spray deodorizer on our lives. We cannot continue to say, "Well, I'll just go to church today and I'll be better" or "I will ask the minister to pray for me and everything will be fine." No, we must begin to ask ourselves what is making us miserable, and we must examine our hearts until we find out what they hold. We need to start asking ourselves, "What is this really all about?"

Many times, people say, "Well, so-and-so made me mad. You wouldn't believe what he did to me!" I need to tell you today that it is never about what other people do to us. We must "own" our responses. Instead of blaming other people for our bad behavior, we need to start asking ourselves: "Why am I so angry and frustrated most of the time? Why do I get upset so easily? What is going on in my heart that causes me to explode so often? Why do I get angrier than seems appropriate in certain situations? Why am I so insecure that I blow up every time someone tries to give me even the tiniest piece of advice? Why do I get upset every time things don't go according to my plan?"

We have to let God deal with other people. We need to leave them to Him and get busy working with Him in our own lives to learn how to live in a world full of difficult people and still have peace and not allow them to control us. Even if the person who hurts us so often were to go away and leave us alone, someone else would show up to take that role! The answer is not to eliminate challenging people or situations from our lives; the answer is for us to change so we can learn to deal with them and stay calm, cool, and collected.

STOP STUFFING YOUR STUFF

One of the primary ways people avoid dealing with pain is to "stuff it." So often, when people hurt us, we stuff it down deep in our hearts instead of dealing with it—and when we stuff pain for too long, it finally explodes in one big ugly fit of anger. It took me years to understand why I would explode over some seemingly minor situation that certainly was not sufficient cause for my ridiculous behavior. I now know that the explosions came from many negative emotions I had stuffed deep inside and was refusing to deal with. The "incident" that seemed to be the problem was just the trigger for the explosion that was hidden and ready to go off at any time.

I was ignoring the real problem and blaming my bad behavior on anything and anyone I could. No matter how spiritual I pretended to be on Sunday at church, my family knew the real me. I managed to ignore the problem for years by making excuses and blaming others, but eventually I had to let God "clean out the refrigerator" so to speak and get to the root of the problem.

God uses the truth to set us free (see John 8:32), but it is not the truth about someone else that sets us free; it is the truth about ourselves that we need! Facing truth about myself was very difficult and emotionally painful, but it was also the beginning of my healing. Whatever the truth is, go ahead and admit it. If you're angry, admit it. If you're afraid, admit it. If you are jealous of someone, admit it. Go to God and say, "You know what, God? I know I have a bad attitude. It really stinks and I can smell it. I want to understand why I have this problem with jealousy. What is in me? Would You show me why I have this problem?"

> God uses the truth to set us free (see John 8:32), but it is not the truth about someone else that sets us free; it is the truth about ourselves that we need!

Maybe the Lord will show you immediately what your struggle is. Perhaps you are insecure; maybe you do not know who you are in Christ. You may compare yourself to others too often. Perhaps you suffered a major hurt or disappointment years ago and you have not been willing to forgive or allow God to heal you yet.

Make a commitment to start being honest and owning your feelings; refuse to stuff them and immediately stop making excuses and blaming others for your negative emotions. You will probably have to talk to God a lot, and you may even need to seek help from a trustworthy friend or minister, but whatever you have to do is worth doing if it helps you to be free and enjoy life.

Whatever has hurt, offended, or angered you, determine today that you are going to go through the pain of facing it and dealing with it. A friend of mine who is a pastor told me recently that when he has a day where he feels depressed, impatient, frustrated, or easily upset he asks himself what happened the day before that he has not dealt with. He said God almost always shows him something he did not deal with the previous day and helps him recognize that as the root of his bad behavior.

One night I tossed and turned until almost 5:00 a.m. and finally asked God, "What's wrong? Why can't I sleep?" He immediately brought to my remembrance a situation that occurred the previous day in which I had been unkind to someone and made an excuse to myself rather than apologizing as I should have. As soon as I asked for His forgiveness and determined I would apologize as soon as I could, I was able to go to sleep. Make a habit of asking, "God, what is this mood or attitude really all about?" You may be surprised by some of the things you learn.

In my life, I've had situations and circumstances hurt and anger me, and over a period of time, I learned how to deal with them. I won't tell you that letting myself feel the pain those situations inflicted and making myself confront my hurt and my anger was easy, but it has been the only way for me to overcome and move beyond them. Facing ourselves and taking responsibility for our attitudes and actions is one of the most difficult things we can ever do, but it is also one of the most important.

OWNING MY ANGER

Dave and I married when he was twenty-six years old and I was twenty-three. One day, he began talking about all the fun he enjoyed as a child. Even though his family didn't have much money and his father died as a result of heavy drinking, Dave had happy memories of his childhood. He had a godly mother who prayed for her children and loved them and kept her family together. Her goodness overrode every difficult thing and every bad thing about Dave's younger days. In the course of conversation, Dave made a comment that hit me hard: "I just remember all the fun we had growing up."

When I heard those words, a feeling of deep sadness came over me and I thought, *I cannot ever remember having fun as a child. In fact, I never even got to be a child.* My father always made me feel guilty if I ever tried to play and have fun as a little girl. In our house, laughter was "noise." So when I grew up, all I ever did was work. I actually became a workaholic because I never learned to play and I thought work was the only activity others approved of. As an adult, the more I thought about my past and all the good I was never able to experience in life, the angrier I became without even realizing why.

As I grew older and developed a relationship with God and came to know His Word, I learned Ephesians 6:12: "For we are not wrestling with flesh and blood [contending only with physical opponents], but against the despotisms, against the powers, against [the master spirits who are] the world rulers of this present darkness, against the spirit forces of wickedness in the heavenly (supernatural) sphere." That verse taught me my father was not my enemy. Yes, he was the one who violated me, but he was under the influence of the enemy. He was simply the devil's puppet. I had to stop blaming my father and begin to heal. I had to stop allowing the devil to continue the cycle of pain he had initiated in my life.

When I realized my childhood had been stolen and I could never get it back, I became angry. I was so angry that it came out in ways that made no sense. I finally realized I was not capable of getting my childhood back, but that God's Word promises He would give me double blessing for my former trouble (see Isaiah 61:7). I learned that we don't overcome evil with more evil, but according to Romans 12:21, we overcome evil with good. If I wanted to "get the devil back" for what he stole from me, I needed to spend the rest of my life helping as many people as I could.

I can now say that I am no longer angry and that I have forgiven my father completely. That did not happen overnight; in fact, it was a long, painful process. But I did confront my anger, rather than try to hide it, pretend it did not happen, or act like it was okay. I was able to release my father to let God deal with him and to press through it and get to the place of peace and forgiveness where I am now.

I will never be able to be a child again. My father, who is now deceased, could never repay what he stole from me. He could never compensate for my losses. But God is my Restorer! When I was about fifty years old, I began to learn how to be a child again. I am laughing and smiling and relaxing and having fun. I may not have had a good start in life, but I am going to have a great finish—and that would never be possible without pressing through my anger and learning to forgive.

As believers, we have an enemy. He will oppose us any way he can. My book *Battlefield of the Mind* makes clear that he uses our own thoughts and feelings to come against us. I like to say that the devil sets us up to get upset. The enemy knows we cannot enjoy power if we have no peace. He knows that the love of God cannot flow through us if we are upset. He will always attempt to upset us, but we can learn to stay calm, cool, and collected at all times. The next time something happens that could easily upset you, ask yourself if it is worth it. Will being upset change it? Can you afford to waste your energy being upset? Will it distract you from God's purpose for your life? Every day we are faced with good and evil; we decide which to choose.

USE YOUR SECRET WEAPON

Every time we suffer hurts, injustices, or offenses, we need to remember that people are not our enemies; Satan is our enemy. God has given us a secret weapon, one that is sure to defeat the devil and destroy his strategies and plans. I mentioned it earlier, but I want to stress how truly important and powerful it is. It's found in Romans 12:21: "Do not let yourself be overcome by evil, but overcome (master) evil with good."

You have a secret weapon against the enemy, and he absolutely hates it because he knows he cannot stand against it. I call it a secret weapon because most people miss it. Your weapon is your God-given ability to be good to people who offend you. Your flesh may want revenge, but God says press through your pain by repaying evil with good. This is difficult to do when you are emotionally distraught; it is much easier to do if you can train yourself to remain calm, cool, and collected no matter what the devil is doing.

When I teach on this scripture, someone always says, "But I can't be good to that person who hurt me. I just can't do it!" Yes, you can. As I wrote earlier, God does not ask us to do things without giving us the ability to do them.

When you do not think you can obey Romans 12:21, all you have to do is say, "God, by Your grace and mercy, I am going to be good to that person. I am not going to tell others what he has done to me. I will not speak ill of that person, but I will pray for him, as You want me to. If I see the person who hurt me, I am going to walk right up to him and say hello. I am going to be kind and obey Your Word and overcome evil with good, by Your grace."

You may not have warm, fuzzy feelings toward a person who has hurt you, but as a follower of Jesus Christ, you must deal with your anger in a biblical way. Do that, as an act of your will, and the right feelings will eventually follow.

To me freedom means I am able to make choices about how I will behave and not be a prisoner to negative emotions. I can act according to God's Word instead of reacting to situations. The devil may be alive and well on earth, but he is not going to control me any longer and he has no right to control you either. God is on your side, and that makes you more than a conqueror.

> *Freedom means I am able to make choices about how I will behave and not be a prisoner to negative emotions.*

Strength in Weakness

Sometimes, all it takes is a little teamwork to turn complete failure into phenomenal success. That was the case with Spencer Silver and Art Fry, two chemists who worked at the 3M company during the 1970s.

In an effort to develop a new adhesive stronger than those in use at the time, Silver achieved the opposite result. He created an adhesive that was less sticky than most of 3M's current products and did not dry. It did stick to certain objects but peeled off easily. Silver could not think of a single use for his not-so-sticky adhesive—nor could anyone else. He completely failed to formulate the stronger, stickier glue 3M had hoped to develop.

Four years later, Silver's 3M colleague Art Fry found himself frustrated every Sunday when he sang in his church choir. He liked to place bookmarks in his hymnal to mark the pages of the hymns to be sung each week so he could locate them quickly and without flipping too many pages. Week after week, Fry's bookmarks fell out of his hymnal. He could have taped or glued them—but the adhesives in tape and glue were too strong to keep from damaging his pages when he removed his bookmarks.

One day, Fry remembered that Silver had developed a weak adhesive and applied some of Silver's product to his bookmark. It was exactly what he needed! His bookmarks stuck to his hymnal pages, but lifted off easily and without damaging the paper.

Before long, Fry began using his "bookmarks" for other purposes—attaching notes to files, leaving brief messages for colleagues, or using them to organize papers or notebooks. His co-workers were intrigued and began wanting the little notes with weak adhesive for themselves.

In the late 1970s 3M coined the name Post-it® for Fry's

bookmarks. They tested the product in 1977 and found little interest in the market. But they knew their self-attaching notes represented a stroke of brilliance and they refused to give up. So, in 1979, they launched a massive promotional and consumer sampling effort in an attempt to catch the attention of the American public with their ingenious new product. In 1980, more than ten years after Spencer Silver's apparent failure with weak adhesive, 3M introduced Post-it® notes across America. Today, Spencer Silver's mild adhesive coats little notes of all sizes, shapes, and colors and can be found in homes, offices, and schools around the world.

CHAPTER 15

THE STRENGTH TO SOAR

"Refuse to be average. Let your heart soar as high as it will."

A. W. TOZER

Being a person who never gives up does not mean barely surviving or simply making it through life with no strength or joy at the end of each day. No, there is a quality of strength, a certain kind of victory, a sense of triumph, and a unique passion that accompanies a person who will not quit. Such a determined, persistent, overcoming individual has not only the ability to survive but the power to thrive.

Think again about the eagle. A person who thrives doesn't scratch around the chicken yard with roosters and hens, nor do they behave fearfully, as chickens do. Instead, he or she has the spirit of a conqueror and the strength to rise and soar like a majestic eagle.

LEARNING TO FLY

Deuteronomy 32:11 says: "As an eagle that stirs up her nest, that flutters over her young, He spread abroad His wings and He took them, He bore them on His pinions." I want you to notice the action in this verse: the eagle stirs up her nest, flutters over her young, spreads her wings broadly, and bears her young on her wings.

If we are going to have strength to soar, we need to understand all this verse means. Let me begin by sharing with you about the eagle's nest. The eagle builds its nest high on a rock, with sturdy sections of rock behind and beneath it. The strong foundation of the nest is composed of tree limbs that can be as large as two inches by six feet. An eagle's nest can weigh as much as two tons when complete and can be up to twenty feet deep and eight to ten feet wide.

Once the foundation is laid, the female eagle stops gathering materials for the foundation and stays home to do the "finish work," but the male eagle continues to bring home vines, leaves, animal fur, anything he can find to build and "furnish" the nest. When the nest is nearly complete, the female lays two or three eggs. In preparation for the eaglets to be born, she pulls feathers from her own breast to pad the nest for the babies. Like most mothers, she is willing to suffer herself in order to bring comfort to her babies. While she watches over the eggs, the male eagle brings her all her food and lets her stay in bed. (I am going to suggest that Dave go eagle watching!)

The male eagle continues to collect things for the nest. He may leave the nest one day and return several times with items such as golf balls, tennis balls, old shoes, tin cans, and any kind of shiny metal he can find. If the mother eagle thinks the nest is too crowded with junk, she throws out what she does not want. I probably tell Dave two or three times each week, "Throw that away. We will never use it!" Sometimes I just do it myself when he isn't watching!

Meanwhile, when the time comes for the baby eaglets to be born, they begin to peck on the shells of their eggs with a small, tooth-like appendage on the end of their beaks. The eaglets use this "tooth" to peck and peck and peck and peck and peck until they finally break through the shell.

God puts that kind of determination in the baby eagles from the very beginning. It is necessary because it helps prepare them for the adversities they will face later in their lives. In fact, I have read if a person tries to intervene and help an eaglet break through its tough shell, the baby may die. It needs to have the opportunity to be tenacious and press through the obstacle of its shell in order to live the way God intended. If it doesn't learn to not give up in the face of difficulty, it cannot survive.

The baby eagles spend the first three months of their lives in the comfortable nest their parents have prepared. It's deep; it's wide; it's sturdy; it's cozy. Momma's there; and everything is great. Their lives are easy; they are well cared for.

But the eaglets get a big surprise when they are about twelve weeks old. Their mother suddenly begins to throw all of their toys out of the nest. She gets in the nest and starts beating around with her wings, throwing things overboard and getting rid of them. Next, she begins to pull out all of the comfortable material in the nest—the feathers and the animal fur—and leaves the babies sitting on thorns and sticks. This is what the Bible means when it mentions that the mother eagle "stirs up her nest." The reason she stirs the nest is that she wants her babies to get out and fly. She knows she must teach them to fly or they will not survive.

Before long, the mother eagle becomes more proactive. She actually begins to nudge them out of the nest. The little eaglets, who have no idea how to fly, fall through the sky, probably very frightened. They do not know what is happening to them, and I am sure they do not want to look at the ground that is fast approaching. Soon, though, they hear a *whooooooooosh* as the mother eagle sweeps up under them to catch them.

I can only imagine what a little eagle would say if he could: "Oh! Thank God! Oh, Momma, boy, was I scared. I was wondering if you loved me, but you must love me because you saved my life. I don't know why you did that to me, but can we just go back to the nest, please? I want my toys back."

At that point, the mother eagle takes the babies right back up to the nest and then nudges them out again. She keeps repeating the process, over and over again, until they finally understand that they have no choice but to fly. The mother eagle does this because she loves them and wants them to have the best life they can possibly have. Most baby eagles won't get out of the nest without this push. Similarly, most of us will also choose comfort over challenge unless we have no choice.

Do you feel God is working in your life the same way the mother eagle does with her young? Has He been taking some of your toys away from you lately? Has He been pulling some of the padding out of your nest so you find yourself sitting on prickly branches? Is He making changes in your life that are leaving you uncomfortable? Is He saying to you, "Come on, it is time to fly"?

Sometimes we feel God has dropped us. We do not know what is going on in our lives; we feel as though we are plummeting toward the earth and we dread the crash landing. We must not be tempted to give up in these situations. We cannot allow ourselves to be afraid when we go through situations we do not understand. God is simply trying to teach us how to fly—and before we fall too far, we'll hear it: *whoooooooosh!* He will be there just in time to save us!

PREENING AND PREPARATION

An eagle begins every day sitting on a rock, systematically passing each of his wing feathers (as many as one thousand two hundred on each wing), through his mouth, one by one. He exhales onto each feather and oils it with oil from a special gland located near his tail. This is called preening; it takes about an hour; and it is similar to a steam cleaning. It reconditions, waterproofs, and prepares the eagle's feathers for the flying he will do that day. This preparation is vital to the eagle's survival and ability to function at his optimum capacity.

Some believers never gain the strength to soar because they do not take time to prepare themselves to be their best every day. I don't know about you, but I have to prepare every day before I go out and deal with people or do anything else. The best form of daily preparation for maximum strength is time with God. Nothing will prepare you to face what you have to face at work, at home, in relationships, or in daily life like taking some time to commune with God before your busy day begins.

When I first understood that I needed to prepare myself for every day by spending time with God, some of my children complained. "Every morning you get up and go to your study, Mom. Can't you just act like a normal mother and fix our breakfast once in a while?"

They were teenagers by that time, so they really didn't need help with breakfast. I replied: "Listen, you're old enough to put cereal in a bowl and pour milk on it. And you should be glad I go to my study every morning. You will have a much nicer day if I take this time with God!"

My daughter Sandra, who is thirty-eight years old now, is spending some time with me while I am working on this book. Yesterday morning, I told her I was going to spend my early morning time with the Lord, and she replied, "Are you going to get nice?" We both laughed because we've learned that even something as simple as being nice to others can be impossible without that daily preparation in God's presence and Word.

I know many people feel extremely pressed for time, and the very thought of adding something else to your schedule makes you shudder. I can hear you now: "Well, I have a house full of children and teenagers. How do you expect me to spend time with God?" Or, "I work three jobs. How do you expect me to spend time with God?"

All I have to say is, the more you have to do and the busier you are, the more you really need to spend time with God. I do not know how you need to adjust your schedule, but I know the time you give to God is no different than the money you give to God. If you give Him time, He will give it back to you. He is in charge of time; He knows how much time you need to accomplish the things you really need to do, and He can protect and help you manage it if you will spend time with Him.

> *If you give Him time, He will give it back to you. He is in charge of time.*

Stop trying to fit God into your schedule and make a decision to put Him first; then work the rest of your schedule around Him.

You don't have to live life feeling as though you'll go over the edge any minute or thinking you simply cannot make it one more day. If you're in a difficult marriage, the best thing you can do for yourself, before you do anything else, is spend time with God right away, every day. If your job entails great responsibility and high stress, the best thing you can do for yourself is to take some of your lunch break, get in your car, and spend time with God. If you have a child who is challenging to raise and hard to deal with, spending time with God before you begin your day will be the best investment you can make. Taking a few five-minute "spiritual vacations" throughout the day is also helpful. Pause for even a few minutes and pray or meditate on scriptures that encourage and strengthen you.

Life does not have to overwhelm you or catch you off guard. Prepare yourself for the challenges you will face each day, and prepare yourself to soar with the eagles by taking time to be with God every day.

COME UP HIGHER

In addition to spending time with God in order to stay strong, eagle Christians also have to be careful to allow the right influences in their lives. Who are you spending time with? Who has input in your life? Who are you listening to?

As I wrote earlier, an eagle who hung out with chickens all the time would surely soon begin to take on some qualities of chickens. Proverbs 4:23 instructs us: "Keep and guard your heart with all vigilance and above all that you guard, for out of it flow the springs of life." Notice these words are a command: "guard your heart." It is your job to guard your heart. Guarding your heart is not something God will do for you.

The very issues of life—the most important things—flow out of your heart, so be very diligent to guard it. On a practical level, this means to be very careful what you allow into your life through the "ear gate" (what you listen to), and through "the eye gate" (what you look at and watch).

Be very careful who you spend time with, and remember, an eagle does not fly with all kinds of other birds, so you cannot hang around with just any group of people. If you spend time with negative people, you will develop a negative attitude. On the other hand, if you surround yourself with those who are positive, you will find your attitude becoming more optimistic. If you spend time with stingy people, you are going to get stingy; but if you hang out with givers, their attitudes and actions will challenge you to come up higher and be more generous.

We need to be the kind of people who *want* to be challenged by others, because that helps us maintain our strength to soar. Let me encourage you to pray for God to put people in your life whose behavior will convict you to live at a higher level. God wants all of us to come up higher. I believe we should live with the goal of never giving up or being content where we are, but to always be pressing forward to come up higher and move to the next level in our faith and in our lives.

BUILD YOUR SPIRITUAL MUSCLES

God wants you to be strong enough to soar over the storms of life and to fulfill all the plans He has for you. For that to happen, you have to build spiritual muscles. You cannot simply *wish* you had spiritual muscles; you have to *build* them just as you have to build muscles in your physical body.

It would be great if we could develop muscles by taking a pill or having someone pray for us. Everyone would want those prayers! We all know that is a silly idea because the only way to develop muscles is to work out!

I always said I would *never* be the kind of person to go to a gym three times a week because I hated exercise! I was okay if I was doing an activity I liked such as walking or golfing (and happened to be getting exercise while I was doing it); but I didn't care much for the whole "let's just exercise" routine. As I mentioned earlier, I now go to the gym three times a week to work out. What made me change my mind? I finally wanted to be stronger, be healthier, and have more energy. That was enough to make me do what I needed to obtain my desired goal.

I'll tell you exactly what happened. God spoke to my heart and said, *You need to do something now so you'll be strong for the last third of your journey.* He wants me to have strength to soar.

I believe I am in the "last trimester" of my ministry, and I want to give birth to everything God has planned for me. In order to travel internationally, do conferences, and fulfill my other responsibilities, I have to have a strong body to house my spirit.

I found a coach and started working out. I started with five-pound weights, and at first I thought I would never be able to lift them. Then I went to seven and a half, then to ten, then to twelve and a half, then to fifteen. Now I can lift twenty pounds easily and sometimes even twenty-five, depending on the exercise I am doing.

It only took nine weeks to work up to this level. You will be amazed at the progress you make if you'll simply be willing to start doing whatever God is leading you to do. It may not be lifting weights, but I am sure He is dealing with you about something because God is always urging us upward. Doing the difficult things God asks is what helps us build spiritual muscle.

Difficult situations, ones that are hard to bear, are the ones that give you strength to soar, so do not run away from them. You will reach the point where circumstances that were once very difficult for you become easy. In fact, you rise above the storms of life, just as the eagle does.

> *Difficult situations, ones that are hard to bear, are the ones that give you strength to soar, so do not run away from them.*

The Gilded Cage

Many times when we think of people who refused to give up, we think of those who overcame obstacles such as poverty or economic disadvantage, physical or mental handicaps, or some other kind of tragic circumstance. But this is not always the case. People born to lives of privilege have challenges too, as we learn from the life of Florence Nightingale.

She was named after the city in which she was born—Florence, Italy—in 1820. The daughter of wealthy parents who had enjoyed a two-year honeymoon in Europe after their wedding, Florence Nightingale was expected to pursue the interests of the privileged, marry well, and live the traditional life of a sophisticated upper-class Englishwoman.

But Florence had other plans. In 1837, in the garden of her family's Hampshire home, she received a "call" from God, in which she sensed Him calling her to do His work, but she did not know specifically what He wanted her to do. Eventually, she realized she was supposed to be a nurse, but her parents felt nursing was "beneath" Florence because of her social background, academic ability, vivacious personality, and beauty. In their opinion, a woman of such distinction should not even consider such a "low class" occupation, and they refused to allow Florence to seek the training she needed to follow her God-given desire to become a nurse.

After considerable conflict in the family, Florence's parents eventually but reluctantly agreed to allow her to take a three-month course in nurse's training. This positioned her to become superintendent of a women's hospital in London in 1853.

In March 1854, the Crimean War broke out when Britain, France, and Turkey declared war on Russia. British newspapers soon reported that wounded soldiers were unable to receive proper medical care because of inadequate medical facilities on the front. A British official and acquaintance of Florence's asked her to oversee the process of staffing military hospitals in Turkey with female nurses who could provide proper care for the men injured in battle. She arrived in Turkey with thirty-eight nurses ready for duty in November 1854.

At first, doctors did not want the nurses working with them and refused to ask for their help. But within days, the medical needs of wounded soldiers overwhelmed the doctors and they recognized the importance and value of having the nurses assist them. As a result of Florence's work, military hospital conditions improved dramatically and mortality rates dropped significantly. Florence earned the deep respect of British soldiers not only for her skills as a nurse and administrator but also for her kindness and compassion to them.

Florence won many prestigious awards throughout her lifetime and made invaluable contributions to the modern health care system, and her influence extends throughout the nursing profession to this day. She raised nursing to an admirable occupation for women and wrote classic books on nursing, books that are still in print.

Florence Nightingale had to overcome enormous family opposition and social pressure to do what she believed God called her to do. She never gave up on His plan for her life and stayed faithful to it until her death at age ninety. Like Florence, be willing to risk the disapproval of others to follow God and stay committed to everything He asks you to do.

CHAPTER 16

NEVER GIVE UP ON YOUR FUTURE

"My interest is in the future because I am going to spend the rest of my life there."
CHARLES F. KETTERING

Throughout this book I've been urging you to never give up. Never giving up means marching into your future with boldness and confidence, seeing each new day as an opportunity to move forward in all the best God has for you and taking each new challenge as a mountain to be climbed instead of a boulder that will crush you.

You have a great future ahead of you, but you will not be able to fully enter into it and enjoy it if your past still holds you captive. The past has the potential to keep you from experiencing the joy, freedom, and blessings of the present and the future—*if you let it*. God wants you to break free from your past and set your face toward your future with hope, courage, and expectation. And the best way I know to never give up on your future is to refuse to be trapped in your past.

DON'T LOOK BACK

God is serious about setting you free from your past. Perhaps no story in the Bible better illustrates this than the unfortunate account of Lot's wife. Let me remind you.

A man named Lot and his family lived in a city consumed by wickedness and sin. God was angry at the degradation in that city and one nearby, so He decided to destroy them. He sent two angels to Lot's house to tell him to take his family and flee. The angels warned them: "Escape for your life! *Do not look behind you* or stop anywhere in the whole valley; escape to the mountains [of Moab], lest you be consumed" (Genesis 19:17, emphasis mine). Lot's wife made the mistake of disobeying the command to not look back. Right then and there, she turned into a pillar of salt.

Jesus did not want us to forget what happened to this woman. Luke 17:32 is a very short Bible verse in which Jesus spoke only three words: "Remember Lot's wife." That was His way of saying: "Stop looking back. The past is finished. Don't look behind you; look to the future ahead!"

As long as I thought and talked about my past, I felt I had no future. God was providing one, but I would have totally missed it had I not finally understood I had to "let go in order to go on!"

Sometimes when we focus on our past, we can't even see our future. We become discouraged, hopeless, and depressed. Don't behave as if your past is more important than your future by giving it too much of your time. If you do, it will keep you trapped in days gone by and steal your enjoyment of the present moment and your hope for the future. When Lot's wife looked back, she lost her life. She lost her family, and she lost her future. I want you to know: you can be destroyed by looking back! You probably will not turn into a pillar of salt, but you can become as "dead" as a pile of salt on the inside if you allow excessive focus on the past to steal the life you have today.

NEW EVERY MORNING

Holding on to your past only gives you opportunity to relive it. The Bible says that as a man thinks so is he (see Proverbs 23:7). I like

to make this point by saying, "Where the mind goes the man follows." If I put my mind on the past, I will keep repeating it one way
or another, but if I put it on the future I will make progress toward
God's dream for me.

You don't have to be afraid of repeating the past. If you believe
God is greater than your sins, mistakes, and shortcomings, you will
have the spiritual energy and the strength and the grace of God to
help you do better in the future. The dreams of your future have
no room for the disappointments of the past. They will keep you
weighted down and stuck.

Many times, before your feet even hit the floor in the mornings,
the enemy begins to remind you of everything you did wrong the
previous day or everything that did not work out well. In doing so,
the enemy's goal is to use yesterday to keep you from living today.
He always wants to use your past against you. But God does not want
us living under the tyranny of the past. Every day can be a new
beginning if we allow it. God's mercy is greater than yesterday's mistakes.

> The enemy's goal is to use
> yesterday to keep you from
> living today.

God's mercies are new every
single day! So every morning when you wake up and
Satan starts reading you an inventory of yesterday's failures, you
need to say aloud: "God's mercies are new every morning. I receive
Your mercy right now, God. I thank You for forgiveness. Thank You
for putting my past behind me and calling me forward into a great
future." Instead of wondering what terrible thing will happen before
the end of the day, start the day by saying, "Something good is going
to happen to me today!"

Chances are, the enemy will be there to whisper to you, "Well,
you will just be disappointed and you won't do any better today than
you did yesterday"; but you can say, "I don't know exactly what the
day holds, but I am going to have a positive attitude. I am going to

press forward and do my best, and at the end of this day, I will get over the mistakes I make and get ready for the next new day. You might as well leave me alone, devil, I will never give up on the new mercies God gives me every morning and I refuse to be trapped in my past." You will be amazed at how much some good positive self-talk will help and even energize you. Being negative drains us all, but faith, hope, and a positive attitude open the door for God to work miracles.

You are the only one who can silence the enemy when he rehearses the past. No one can do it for you. If you are determined to overcome him and to press into the wonderful future God has for you, you will need to learn to talk back to the devil. You cannot borrow someone else's determination; you have to dig down deep and get a firm grip on your inner strength and say: "I will not give up! The enemy will not use my past to steal my future! I am not going to let yesterday affect today!"

Fulfilling your destiny demands letting go of what lies behind. I had to stop mourning over what I had lost and take an inventory of what I had left. I offered that to God, even though it did not seem like much, and He has done wonderful things in my life. He will do the same thing for you if you will work with Him instead of against Him. God called Himself "I AM" (see Exodus 3:14). He said that was His name. Why? What kind of a name is that? He is making a strong point that He is ever present, ready to work in our lives right now. He is with us to help us right now! He is able to make even past mistakes work to our benefit if we trust Him. Will you let go of the past and live every day fully while you press into your future?

FORGET THE FORMER THINGS

The prophet Isaiah urges us to forget the past: "Do not [earnestly] remember the former things; neither consider the things of old" (Isaiah 43:18). Remembering and considering are processes of the mind, so Isaiah is basically saying: "Get your mind off your *old* sins, your *old* failures, your *old* mistakes, your *old* friends, your *old* life, the *old* nature, your *old* job—everything about your past. Do not let your mind dwell on such "former things.""

After I left the job in which I taught well-attended Bible studies at a church and was leading Joyce Meyer Ministries, people who remembered the Bible studies occasionally asked: "Don't you miss the good old days when we were all together at the church for Bible study? Weren't those good times?"

Yes, those were good days. They were so important to the development of the ministry I have today, and we did have wonderful times studying the Word together. But I have to say I really don't miss those times. They were good days, but the days I am living now are better! If we miss the "old days" long enough and keep thinking about them and talking about them, we will completely think ourselves out of the ability to enjoy today or the future.

I don't know exactly what God has in His plan for me, but I do know it will be good. I am excited about walking it out with Him, and in order to do that I have to refuse to allow my mind to "drift" into directions that will not benefit me. Do your own thinking on purpose, and don't just wait to see what happens to fall into your mind.

We see things with our mind. What do you see? After Abraham had endured a great loss, God led him to a mountaintop. He told him to look north, south, east, and west and then said, "You can have whatever you see!" (see Genesis 13:14–17). Wow! That sounds like a good plan to me. Why look back and get more of what we have had when we can look forward and enjoy things too wonderful for us to even imagine?

As we continue reading in Isaiah 43, God says: "Behold, I am doing a new thing! Now it springs forth; do you not perceive and know it and will you not give heed to it? I will even make a way in the wilderness and rivers in the desert" (v. 19).

Notice, God does not say, "I *will* do a new thing"; He says, "I *am doing* a new thing." God is doing a new thing, but to experience it, you have to turn your focus away from what God did in the past, and onto what He is doing now. Failing to do this will result in a life full of regret.

To regret means "to feel sorry or to grieve over; to mourn; a sense of loss and longing for something or someone gone; distress over desire unfulfilled or an action performed or not performed." Regret binds you to your past and keeps you focused on former things. But God is doing a new thing *now*. Be a person who lets go of past regrets, lives in the present, and never gives up on a fabulous future.

> *Be a person who lets go of past regrets, lives in the present, and never gives up on a fabulous future.*

I do not believe God releases the blessings He allots for us each day if we live in the past. He knows we will not enjoy them if we are stuck in a memory fifteen years old or if we cannot get past a mistake we made in high school. Come into the present; receive the blessings God has for you today, and look forward to the future with great anticipation.

GOD FORGETS!

Do you really believe God forgets your sins once you repent? He does. Elsewhere in this book, I mentioned that Jesus paid in full the price for our sins, that we are forgiven and have no reason to feel guilty or condemned once we have repented. Now I want to go a step further and make sure you understand God not only *forgives* but also *forgets* all your sins. He does not forgive you and then say: "Oh boy, I remember when I had to forgive Johnny for pulling his sister's hair and making her cry. Now he wants me to forgive him for cheating on his algebra test. His list of forgiven sins is getting awfully long!" No, if Johnny were to say to God, "I know You've already forgiven me for pulling my sister's hair a couple of years ago, but now I need Your forgiveness for cheating on a test," God would say, "Your sister's hair? You asked me to forgive you for that? I have absolutely no recollection of that; there's no record of it anywhere. Now, what did you want to tell Me about your algebra test?"

In both the Old and New Testaments, God makes sure we understand how completely He forgets our sins. In Jeremiah 31:34 He says: "For I will forgive their iniquity, and I will [seriously] remember their sin no more." In Hebrews 10:17, the writer references Jeremiah's words: "And their sins and their lawbreaking I will remember no more."

I want us to see this verse in context:

> *For by a single offering He has forever completely cleansed and perfected those who are consecrated and made holy. And also the Holy Spirit adds His testimony to us [in confirmation of this]. For having said, This is the agreement (testament, covenant) that I will set up and conclude with them after those days, says the Lord: I will imprint My laws upon their hearts, and I will inscribe them on their minds (on their inmost thoughts and understanding), He then goes on to say, And their sins and their lawbreaking I will remember no more (vv. 14–17).*

This passage is not talking about a forgiveness that happens the day we receive Christ and takes care of all of our *previous* sins. God's forgiveness is ongoing for the duration of our lives; it is for every day. When Jesus died on the cross two thousand years ago, He not only forgave everything we had done in our pasts, but He also committed Himself to forgive every sin we would commit in the future. He knows our thoughts before we think them; He knows our words before they come out of our mouths; He knows every wrong decision we will ever make—and it's all already covered. All we have to do is stay in relationship with Him. After all, what He wants from us more than anything else is not perfect performance, perfect behavior, or perfect attitudes, but hearts that really love Him. Always remember, God is not surprised by our bad behavior. He knew about it long before we did and He wants us anyway. He is excited about helping us grow into all He knows we can be.

God buries our sins—past, present, and future—in the sea of forgetfulness and remembers them no more. Often, we preach God's forgiveness, but we fail to focus on the fact that He also forgets them. "I will remember your sins no more!" says God. Determine today to stop remembering what God has forgotten.

Throughout this book, I have mentioned many of the devastating and dysfunctional situations of my past, and for years I allowed the impact of those circumstances to keep me from moving forward into my future. I did not progress into the new life God had for me because I kept using my past as an excuse to continue in old thought patterns and behaviors.

Jesus said, "And you will know the Truth, and the Truth will set you free" (John 8:32). When we are willing to face the truth about ourselves, we will be set free. When I accepted the fact that I was blaming other people and the circumstances of my past for my failure to go forward into the future, I was finally able to take responsibility for my life, deal with my past, and become free to pursue my future. I found the strength to believe 2 Corinthians 5:17: "Therefore if any person is [ingrafted] in Christ (the Messiah) he is a new creation (a new creature altogether); the old [previous moral and spiritual condition] has passed away. Behold, the fresh and new has come!"

Being a new creation in Christ does not mean all your problems and weaknesses vanish into thin air the minute you make a commitment to live for God. It means you become brand-new spiritual "clay." Let me explain.

Jesus, who is called "the Seed," comes to live in us as the seed of Almighty God, bringing with Him a seed of everything God is. In the physical world, seeds must be planted; they need time to become rooted and grounded; and they must be nurtured. They need sun-light and water. Someone has to keep the weeds from choking the life out of them and hindering their growth.

A similar process is necessary in our spiritual lives. We do not become "new creations" overnight, but through a process. God's Word needs to be planted in our hearts, and it needs time to take root in us. We need the water of God's Word (see Ephesians 5:26) and the light of His Spirit to strengthen us. It is also extremely help-ful to take advantage of every opportunity we have to be nurtured by more mature believers who can guide us.

As we continue and continue and continue in these good, godly habits, those seeds God planted in us begin to grow up like plants and become trees of righteousness (see Isaiah 61:3). Over time, we realize we are changing not because of our own effort but because we are spending time with God and growing in His Word. As we dwell in His presence and live by His truth, His image is re-created in us and we truly become new.

THE PAST IS PAID FOR

The enemy loves to remind you of your past. He takes the mistakes, disappointments, hurts, and offenses from former seasons in your life and replays them in your mind like broken records. In between every verse of those same old songs, he sings this chorus: "Now you have to pay. You have to pay for everything you did wrong. You have to pay! You have to pay! You have to pay!"

As I mentioned earlier, many people believe the lie that we some-how need to compensate for the misjudgments or wrongdoings of our pasts. I do not want you to fall into this trap. Let me urge you not to ever try to "pay" for your past by giving up your future. Do not believe the lie that a bad past disqualifies you for a great future. Do not allow yourself to believe you have made so many mistakes in the past that you have no hope for the future.

In Jeremiah 29:11, God says: "For I know the thoughts and plans that I have for you, says the Lord, thoughts and plans for welfare and peace and not for evil, to give you hope in your final outcome." No matter what your past may hold, determine in your heart to believe that God has good plans for you. Your mistakes cannot change this truth. The only way it would not be true in your life would be for you to reject it. If you are not willing to believe it, you are not likely to see it come to pass for you. But if you will believe it and not stop believing it, you will soon see God's thoughts and plans toward you are for your welfare and peace, not for evil, regardless of your past. He is for you; He has great plans for you; and you have every reason to have hope for your future.

He Stuck with It

You may never have heard of Thomas Adams, but you have probably enjoyed the product developed as a result of his persistence. Let me explain.

During the 1860s, success seemed impossible for Adams. After failing at several jobs and trades, he became a photographer. He was creative and enjoyed his work, but struggled to make a living at it.

About the same time, Mexican general Antonio de Santa Anna went into exile in the United States and stayed at Adams's home in Staten Island, New York. Santa Anna encouraged the innovative Adams to see what he could do with chicle, a substance derived from the sapodilla trees of Mexico. Santa Anna believed the chicle might be used to make synthetic rubber and told Adams he could secure the substance for him at very little cost from friends in Mexico.

So Adams went to work experimenting with chicle in a warehouse in New York City. He tried mixing it with rubber to make bicycle tires, but failed. He also tried to make toys, masks, rain boots, and other items, but he never succeeded. After experimenting diligently for about a year and finding no use for chicle, he decided to throw his remaining chicle stock in the East River and forget about it.

Before he disposed of the chicle, he paid a visit to a local drugstore, where he overheard a little girl asking to buy a piece of chewing gum for a penny. At that time, chewing gum in America was made from paraffin wax. In that moment, Adams realized he could probably make chewing gum from chicle, not realizing this had been taking place in Mexico for years. That night, Adams and his son made pieces of chewing gum from chicle—little pieces without any artificial flavors—and wrapped them in brightly colored tissue papers. They sold each stick of gum for a penny.

Adams finally found success selling his gum, which he called "Adams' New York Gum Number 1." In 1888, his "Tutti-Frutti" gum became the first to be sold in vending machines and by the end of the nineteenth century, he had established the most profitable chewing gum company in America. His company gained a monopoly in the chewing gum business in 1899 when it merged with the six largest chewing gum manufacturers in the United States and Canada. This company developed and sold Chiclets®, with tremendous success, beginning in the early 1900s.

Next time you see a package of chewing gum, remember Thomas Adams and let it remind you to never give up.

CHAPTER 17

THE POWER OF HOPE

"Hope is necessary in every condition."
SAMUEL JOHNSON

On Christmas Eve 1981, a group of people embarked on a tragic journey they would never forget. A woman named Pat, her husband Gary, her two teenage stepsons, and a close friend were flying to Colorado to go skiing. Gary was piloting the small plane that was to get them to their destination. He had his pilot's license but had not yet been instrument certified, so he did not file a flight plan.

Flying over the mountains taxed the small engine, and they began to go down. Gary saw a tiny clearing along the tree line in the middle of the mountain range. He aimed for it and although they crash-landed, he was able to keep much of the plane intact and right side up.

The impact of the crash broke Pat's back, but everyone else's injuries were minimal. Pat was unconscious for a while, but she vaguely remembers her husband saying that he was leaving to get help.

The four stayed in the cramped cabin of the plane and waited overnight for help to arrive. The next day they thought their prayers had been answered. About a hundred yards away a military helicopter landed and a group of soldiers jumped out. The stranded passengers thought their ordeal was over. They assumed Gary had made it to safety and that this was their rescue. A few minutes later the group realized the men were *not* looking for crash victims. Horrified, they screamed for help, but the helicopter engine was so deafening the soldiers could not hear them. The white top of the plane blended into the snow; the snow was too deep for the boys to make it very far away from the plane, and they had nothing to use as a signal. There was nothing else they could do. The helicopter took off. The cold silence of the mountain crushed their spirits.

The victims ate snow for Christmas dinner and tried to build a fire, to no avail. They sat in the freezing temperature and endured the pitch-blackness of night. In the back of Pat's mind, she asked God, *If we are all going to die, can I go first? I can't watch the others die in front of me.*

Thankfully, they had a Bible with them. Through it, the Lord began to encourage them to press on when it seemed there was no hope.

Because no flight plan was filed, no one knew the group was missing. However, the emergency transponder was sending out a signal. Little did the crash victims know a commercial jet flying overhead heard the signal, but since there was no report of a missing plane, it was assumed that the transponder was being used as a drug drop. (In the 1980s, drug traffickers dropped loads of drugs packed with transponders so teams on the ground could locate them.) However, when the same flight heard the transponder a couple of days later, the alert went out and hundreds of people began to search the mountains. It was difficult to pinpoint the location of the transponder because the signal echoed off the mountains.

The weather grew worse the sixth day; a blizzard was setting in. But then the cold and hungry survivors began to hear noises outside. Suddenly out of nowhere a man with a big smile appeared in the window of the plane! Reinforcements were called in. Even against orders a helicopter pilot landed his Huey on a jagged sheet of ice in blizzard conditions. Pat and the boys were loaded on the helicopter, but their friend would have to be skied down the next morning. The snow was chest deep now, so a team of rescuers with emergency supplies stayed with him overnight. The next morning it took seven hours to ski him to a landing zone.

Pat had surgery on her broken back and to this day has a steel rod helping to hold her back together. The boys both lost about half of each foot due to frostbite, and the friend lost both of his legs at the knee.

For months, no one had seen or heard from Gary. Pat knew he was gone.

It took several months, but Pat began to make a strong recovery. She was encouraged to press on. She began to feel God had something for her to do. She realized she could either feel sorry for herself and live as a victim, or go on with life.

Nine months after the accident, Gary's body was discovered. He had apparently fallen into a ravine and frozen to death.

Pat decided to press on and find the work God was calling her to do. She went through a decade of searching and emotional wilderness, trials, and pain—all in preparation for the work she now does with a man she married after Gary's death.

Always remember that you have two choices when you find yourself in difficult circumstances: you can give up or go on! Only you can make the choice, but if you choose to go on you can encourage many others throughout your life who are faced with the same choice you once had to make.

> *You have two choices when you find yourself in difficult circumstances: you can give up or go on!*

HOLD ON TO YOUR HOPE

Pat and the other plane crash survivors learned how to hope in a seemingly hopeless situation. People like Pat, who have seen God's faithfulness in the past, tend to be very hopeful. They know a bad situation can turn into a wonderful testimony in a matter of minutes. They know how to hold on to hope and refuse to give up.

People who have lost hope view life from the perspective of dread.

Dread, which is closely related to fear, steals the ability to enjoy ordinary life and makes people anxious about the future. It keeps them from looking forward to the next hour, the next day, the next month, or the next decade. Their thoughts about the present are negative and their outlook on the future is filled with fear, pessimism, doubt, and worry.

Hope, on the other hand, is the opposite of dread; and it is a close relative of faith. Hebrews 11:1 tells us faith is "the assurance (the confirmation, the title deed) of the things [we] hope for." When we have hope, our outlook on life and the future is positive. We can have hope because we trust in God's love, His power to provide for us, and His ability to lead us in every situation. Hope keeps us from worrying, allows us to leave our unanswered questions in God's hands, empowers us to stay at peace, and enables us to believe the best about the days to come. People with hope are happy, optimistic, and full of strength and courage.

Because hope is such a powerful force, the enemy goes after it with a vengeance. If he can steal your hope, he can set you on the path toward total despair and depression—and that's his intention. He will plant thoughts such as these in your mind:

- You have always been this way. You will never change.
- No one will ever want to marry you.
- You might as well settle into this entry-level job, because you will never be smart enough to get a promotion.
- You might as well go buy some clothes in a larger size because you will never lose this weight.
- Your children will never amount to anything.
- You will not have enough money for retirement.
- No one in your family has lived more than seventy years, so you cannot expect a long life.
- You will never own a new car.
- You will never own your own home.
- You will never get out of debt.

If you read these statements carefully, you will notice they have a common thread running through them: self-pity! The devil puts thoughts in our minds to make us feel sorry for ourselves and resent the people who have what we are convinced we can never have.

Self-pity is a very destructive negative emotion. Self-pity makes us blind to our blessings and the possibilities before us; it steals our hope for today and for tomorrow. People who pity themselves think, *Why should I try to do anything? I'll just fail.*

I used to love to sit and drink my coffee, feeling sorry for myself and thinking about how mistreated I was. But I finally realized self-pity is idolatry because it is self-focus carried to an extreme and it rejects God's love and ability to change things for us.

I encourage you to be determined to not waste one more day of your life in self-pity. When you lose hope and begin to feel sorry for yourself, stop right that minute and say, "I refuse to feel sorry for myself. I may be in a difficult season of life right now, but I will not stop hoping for better things! The Roman orator Cicero said, "While there's life, there's hope." This is true. As long as you are alive, you have the ability to hope.

The enemy wants you consumed with hopelessness and will tell you all sorts of things about yourself, your life, other people, and God if he thinks you will believe them and lose hope. But the devil is a liar; you must not believe anything he says. The psalmist refused to give up when the enemy assaulted him with hopelessness. He knew how to talk to himself to overcome such attacks, and said, "Why are you cast down, O my inner self? And why should you moan over me and be disquieted within me? *Hope in God* and wait expectantly for Him, for I shall yet praise Him, my Help and my God" (Psalm 42:5, emphasis mine).

Remember, God has thoughts and plans for your good, to give you hope for your future (see Jeremiah 29:11). If you will hold on to your hope and fight for it when the enemy tries to take it away, you will see amazing things take place in your life. Being hopeful helps you to press on instead of giving up.

HOPE IN THE MIDST OF DISAPPOINTMENT

A friend recently told me a story that illustrates what happens when a person refuses to give up hope even after significant disappointment.

A pastor met with a member of his church, a businessman who was very excited and full of faith because God was working in his life in significant ways. The man's business was selling large equipment to companies, and he told his pastor he had recently bid on a very lucrative contract. He believed he would get this contract. In fact, the man was absolutely *convinced* the vendor would give him the business.

The pastor believed God showed him the man would not receive the contract and advised the man to reconsider his expectations so he would not be disappointed when it did not materialize. The man refused, saying, "I *know* I am going to get that contract. I'm believing for it. My faith is strong. I am going to get it."

He did not. The contract went to a competitor.

At first the businessman was upset, but then the pastor gave him some wise advice: "I believe the best course of action at this point is to go talk to the people who gave the contract to someone else and let them know you would be glad to help them and be involved in their business any way you can. Tell them you understand why they bought the equipment from someone else, but that you would like to do the installation because you have the best installers anywhere." He encouraged him to remain hopeful and refuse to be defeated by one setback or disappointment.

The businessman took his pastor's advice and decided to press through his disappointment and not give up hope for a relationship with the company that did not buy from him, even though he would have to accept a different type of relationship than he initially wanted.

He did get the contract for installation and while the businessman's employees were installing the equipment, the head of the company noticed what an excellent job they were doing. The next time he purchased a large piece of equipment, he bought from the businessman—and it was a much, much bigger sale than the first contract would have been. So he ended up with "the best of both worlds" because he refused to stop hoping in the face of a major disappointment.

When things don't work out the way we wish they would, we can either be sad about what we did not get, or we can be creative and look to see what we can do with what is left.

The businessman chose to have a positive, hopeful attitude toward a disappointing situation. He pressed through the temptation to be angry with the company that did not award him the first contract or jealous of the people who did get it, and he ended up with the best deal of all. He thought God would bless him one way—with the first contract—but God rewarded him in another way. First, He blessed him with a profitable business arrangement, and second, He taught him the importance and value of staying hopeful in the aftermath of disappointment.

HOPE WHEN THE HEAT IS ON

One way we develop hope is by learning about how God came through for people in seemingly hopeless situations, such as Pat and the businessman who sold large equipment. The Bible is also full of stories that give us hope and build our faith. One of them is the remarkable account of three young Hebrew men—Shadrach, Meshach, and Abednego—who insisted upon worshipping the one true God and refused to worship a golden image (see Daniel 3:1–6). As punishment for their rejection of the false god, the young men were thrown into a fiery furnace—turned up seven times hotter than its usual temperature. They would be incinerated instantly; their lives were finished; the situation was hopeless.

Was the situation really hopeless? Not with God involved. My favorite part of this story takes place when the king who tried to incinerate them looked into the furnace and saw a fourth man in the furnace with them (many scholars believe him to be the pre-incarnate Jesus), and then realized the chains or ropes with which the young men had been bound had become loose. When the three young men came out of the furnace unharmed, they received promotions in the king's government! Everything about a terrible, seemingly hopeless situation turned out well for them.

Like Shadrach, Meshach, and Abednego, you may be facing a situation that seems utterly hopeless. I urge you today to ask and allow the Lord to restore your hope. Hope simply says, "I believe something good can and will happen." Sadness, disappointment, and despair have to flee in the presence of hope. As long as you have hope, you will not be able to give up.

> *Sadness, disappointment, and despair have to flee in the presence of hope.*

On the Right Track

During his early years, Andrew Carnegie was expected to follow in his father's footsteps and become a weaver in his home country of Scotland. Prior to the industrial revolution, which brought steam-powered looms to Scotland in 1847, a weaver could make a decent living working with his hands. But when mechanized looms arrived, companies no longer needed hand loom weavers. When this happened to Carnegie's father, the family's standard of living dropped dramatically and his mother had to go to work. She opened a grocery store and made extra money mending shoes. Reflecting on those days, Carnegie wrote that that experience taught him "what poverty meant" as he watched his father beg for work. As a result, he wrote: "Then and there came the resolve that I would cure that when I got to be a man." He grew up with the determination to do all he could to provide jobs to hardworking people and to ensure he did not live an impoverished life.

In 1848, Carnegie's mother took a drastic step in an effort to avoid complete devastation and financial ruin for her family. She borrowed money to move herself, her husband, and her children to America. Two of her sisters had already settled in Pittsburgh, so the Carnegie family joined them there. Carnegie and his father both found work in a cotton factory.

Carnegie then took a job in Pittsburgh's telegraph office as a messenger boy. He distinguished himself by working hard and eagerly volunteering for new or additional responsibilities. At the same time, he developed a disciplined reading habit and found ways to see plays and experience other cultural and educational activities.

Through his work at the telegraph office, the diligent young

Carnegie caught the attention of Thomas A. Scott of the Pennsylvania Railroad. Scott soon hired Carnegie as his personal secretary. Through dedication and an outstanding work ethic, Carnegie moved through the ranks at the Pennsylvania Railroad and became Scott's successor as superintendent of the Pittsburgh division.

After the Civil War, Carnegie saw great potential in the iron industry, so he resigned from the railroad and set out to make a fortune in iron. And make a fortune he did. With smart decisions, calculated risks, and a keen eye for disciplined spending, he became one of the wealthiest men and greatest philanthropists of his day.

Carnegie believed "the man who dies rich dies disgraced," so he began giving away money as he grew older, focusing on educational and cultural causes. By the time of his death, he had funded the establishment of two thousand five hundred public libraries and given away approximately 350 million dollars.

Hard work and the relentless pursuit of his goals made Andrew Carnegie, once the impoverished son of an unemployed weaver, a man his peers called "the richest man in the world." He set his mind to becoming a wealthy entrepreneur and one who employed others. By working hard, taking advantage of opportunities, and embracing responsibility, he did it. When you set your mind to the accomplishment of your goals and do what you can to reach them, you will achieve them.

CHAPTER 18

LIKE A SUDDEN WIND

*"The highest reward for a man's toil is not what he gets for it
but what he becomes by it."*

JOHN RUSKIN

I once heard a story called "The Obstacle in Our Path" that I want to share with you.

In ancient times, a king placed a boulder on a roadway. Then he hid himself and watched to see if anyone would remove the huge rock. Some of the king's wealthiest merchants and courtiers came by and simply walked around it.

Many loudly blamed the king for not keeping the roads clear, but none did anything about getting the big stone out of the way. Then a peasant came along carrying a load of vegetables. On approaching the boulder, the peasant laid down his burden and tried to move the stone to the side of the road. After much pushing and straining, he finally succeeded. As the peasant picked up his load of vegetables, he noticed a purse on the road where the boulder had been. The purse contained many gold coins and a note from the king saying that the gold was for the person who removed the boulder from the roadway. The peasant learned what many others never understand.

The important lesson to remember is that work has its rewards. This is true in corporate settings, in your home, in your relationships, and in every area of life. If you are willing to pay the price, you can have the prize. The same principle applies in our spiritual lives as we walk with God. He requires us to work to accomplish what He calls us to do, to fulfill His purposes for our lives, and to follow the dreams He plants in our hearts; and He promises that if we are diligent, we will have a reward.

I believe many people are unhappy today because they only want to commit to things that are easy or convenient. This saddens me because these people often cheat themselves out of the rewards God has for them simply because they want to avoid difficulty. If they would be willing to exert effort, they would reap great benefits.

God wants to bless us in many ways. Sometimes He requires us to do something difficult before we receive certain blessings because He wants those blessings to be rewards for our diligence. There are no rewards for starting something; there are no rewards for quitting. But if we never give up, we *will* receive our rewards.

GOD IS A REWARDER

Perhaps the one verse that most clearly presents the promise that God rewards those who never give up is Hebrews 11:6: "He is the rewarder of those who earnestly and diligently seek Him [out]."

We must believe God is a *rewarder* of those who diligently seek Him. If we are diligent, we can expect rewards. We cannot manipulate God; we must believe His Word and do what He asks us to do. He tells us the diligent will be blessed, so we simply keep on keeping on and refuse to give up.

You know by now that doing something the right way one time does not necessarily bring great reward. It is doing what is right over and over and over and over that will bring the good result you desire. You must be diligent when everyone else around you slacks off or gives up. Diligence is not easy, but it has its rewards—and I guarantee you, they are worth every effort and every sacrifice you make.

THE WORK BEHIND THE REWARDS

There is no such thing as a "drive-through" breakthrough! You can get a drive-through hamburger or a drive-through milkshake; you can even drop off and pick up your dry cleaning at a drive-through, but you do not have the option of drive-through convenience if you want a reward from God. There are no shortcuts with Him. If you want the reward, you have to do the work.

At this season of my life, I am living in the rewards that come with years of diligence—not one year, not two years, not even ten years, but *decades* of diligence. Knowing I have obeyed God and followed His call on my life is the most important reward, and being able to live my dream of ministering to others is an added benefit. It thrills me to realize that although I did not have a great beginning in life due to the devil's attack, I am having a great finish and God has been exalted as King.

I want to remind you that I did not see rewards quickly. For many years I actually felt that I was doing all I knew to do and still not making much progress. Actually, I was making progress, but there were so many things in my life that needed fixing I couldn't get past what was still wrong in order to see what had changed for the better. I want you to know this so you will not be discouraged if you struggle with similar feelings. Most of the time, you really are making progress when you do not think you are moving forward even one inch. God is working in you and moving you along, little by little, in such a way that you may not even notice you are no longer where you were last year. But God notices; and He wants you to keep going, even if you only advance one inch at a time. The Bible says God delivers us from our enemies little by little (see Deuteronomy 7:22). Merely refusing to give up is a victory in itself.

> *God is working in you and moving you along, little by little, in such a way that you may not even notice you are no longer where you were last year.*

THERE'S A REASON FOR THOSE BLESSINGS

When we see people who seem to be showered with God's blessings and are prospering in life, people who appear perfectly at peace and are always joyful and seem to have everything work out in their favor, we wonder why they live such blessed lives. The world calls them lucky, but we know better. We know there is reason for the good life they now enjoy.

Most of the time, people we refer to as "blessed" did not start their lives in a blessed state. They have had their share of challenges and adversities; they have gone through difficulties; they have been diligent to live by God's Word; they have stayed faithful to Him; they have given to others when they had little to give; they have prayed when they did not feel like praying; and they have been patient, loving, and kind to people when they did not want to be nice to anyone. They did these things in obedience to God's Word, and because they knew doing them would bring joy to their lives.

When God saw that these people made wise decisions, followed Him wholeheartedly, and refused to give up over a period of time, He blessed them. He is a God who loves to bless us, but He does test us to see if we are determined and willing to live for Him even when we don't get what we would like.

In Matthew 5, Jesus says the pure in heart are blessed (see v. 8), but we must remember that becoming pure in heart is not easy or quick. He also says that the makers and maintainers of peace are blessed (see v. 9); but peacemaking and peacekeeping require humility, sacrifice, and a willingness to adapt and adjust to other people. God's blessings are provided freely by His grace, but we must be willing to obey Him if we want to enjoy them.

I have been through many difficult situations no one knows about. I had a lot of lonely times, and a lot of hard years. I endured many years of rejection and judgment and criticism as a woman in ministry. But now I have the reward. It was not easy, but it is worth it.

Your reward will come too if you will refuse to give up! I shudder to think what my life would be like now had I given up during one of those times I was so tempted to quit. I thank God that He kept pushing me forward and sometimes even dragging me while I was kicking and screaming about every inconvenience. At times, I felt as if I could not go backward; I didn't know how to go forward, but God would not let me quit. He provided people to help, money to pay bills, open doors, strength, wisdom, and everything else I needed. The road was narrow, steep, and difficult to climb, but I eventually realized it was the only road that was truly going anywhere. I am so glad now that I did not give up, and if you refuse to give up, your reward will come also.

TO THOSE WHO OVERCOME...

We have said that even though we like to be thought of as strong, determined, and able to overcome difficulties, we still try to avoid obstacles, opposition, and adversities that will eventually give us what we say we want. We can receive much encouragement from the book of Revelation because it is full of promises of rewards for those who overcome:

> He who is able to hear, let him listen to and give heed to what the Spirit says to the assemblies (churches). To him who overcomes (is victorious), I will grant to eat [of the fruit] of the tree of life, which is in the paradise of God (Revelation 2:7).

> He who overcomes (is victorious), I will make him a pillar in the sanctuary of My God; he shall never be put out of it or go out of it, and I will write on him the name of My God and the name of the city of My God, the new Jerusalem, which descends from My God out of heaven, and My own new name (Revelation 3:12).

He who overcomes (is victorious), I will grant him to sit
beside Me on My throne, as I Myself overcame (was victori-
ous) and sat down beside My Father on His throne (Revela-
tion 3:21).

These scriptures remind us of our heavenly reward when we overcome adversity with faith, perseverance, and character. We gain victory in our lives when we choose to embrace the difficult path of
overcoming.

SQUEEZE THROUGH THE NARROW PLACE

If you want to reach any worthy goal at all or do anything significant for God, you will find you always have to go through a narrow
place. Any time God leads you toward a broader place—a position
of greater influence, greater enjoyment in life, or a fulfilled desire—
you will have to squeeze through a narrow place. Your narrow place
may be a time when you have to walk away from negative relationships, when you have to discipline your mouth to speak positively
instead of complaining, or when you have to put yourself on such
a tight budget you can no longer afford some of the small pleasures
of life, such as a cup of gourmet coffee or a movie ticket. You may
have to choose to work while others are entertaining themselves.
These kinds of disciplines will squeeze you and press you, but they
will also lead you to the broad places and blessings God has for you.
When you are pressed and squeezed to the point you feel you can
hardly breathe, make sure you stay focused on the reward ahead. It
is like working all week and looking forward to payday on Friday.
When the devil tries to discourage you, just say aloud, "Payday is
coming!"

Jesus spoke of the narrow gate in Matthew 7:13–14: "Enter through
the narrow gate; for wide is the gate and spacious and broad is the
way that leads away to destruction, and many are those who are

entering through it. But the gate is narrow (contracted by pressure) and the way is straitened and compressed that leads away to life, and few are those who find it."

Many people never leave the broad road that leads to destruction. Why? Because there's plenty of room on the broad road. You will have plenty of company on the broad road. It is the easy way. Jesus calls it "spacious," and when I think of that, I think of a person who has room to carry all their fleshly baggage with them on that road! The broad road may be easy and wide, but it does not lead to anything good. In fact, it leads to destruction.

Those who really want to find life must follow what Jesus calls the "compressed" way. It's straight; it's narrow; it's not as easy to walk as the broad road. When we decide to walk that narrow path, God begins requiring more of us. He starts taking away some of our fleshly baggage. He pulls the padding out of our nest. He asks us to let go of some of our old ways, to adjust some of our attitudes, to raise the standards in our relationships and conversations, and to make some changes in the ways we spend our time and money. Living on the narrow path requires that we let God out of the "Sunday Morning Box" we often try to keep Him in and invite Him into every day and everything. We cannot have any places in our lives where God is not welcome.

Everything God asks us to do as we walk the narrow way may not be easy, but it will be good for us. It may not feel like a blessing as we go through it, but it leads to blessing in the end. It will require us to overcome some things, but it will lead us to wonderful rewards.

I encourage you to get on the narrow road and stay there. There may not be many people on it with you, but if you look carefully you will see Jesus because the narrow way is always the road He travels. Do not go back to the broad road when the narrow one loses its appeal. The broad road is deceptive. It may be fun for a while, it may be easy, but it leads to trouble. Pay the price to stay with God on the road that leads to life.

PAYDAY IS COMING

The promise of reward is one dynamic that keeps us moving in the right direction and refusing to quit through hard times. When you become discouraged or weary as you press through, do not give up, because the price you pay is worth it in the end. Payday is coming!

God may be giving you some tough assignments right now. He may be asking you to do some things you feel you absolutely cannot do, but I want you to know: if you will press in and press on and press through, God has a reward for you. The promise of reward is awesome. It keeps us motivated and encouraged.

A scripture that immediately comes to my mind when I think about the rewards God promises when we never give up is Hebrews 11:6, which tells us God "is the rewarder of those who earnestly and diligently seek Him [out]." We must always remember that God rewards those who diligently seek Him. His rewards may not come in the form you expect or at the time you expect, but they will come.

> *His rewards may not come in the form you expect or at the time you expect, but they will come.*

One of my favorite passages of scripture is Isaiah 61:7–8: "Instead of your [former] shame you shall have a twofold recompense; instead of dishonor and reproach [your people] shall rejoice in their portion. Therefore in their land they shall possess double [what they had forfeited]; everlasting joy shall be theirs. For I the Lord love justice."

Look with me at the first part of the passage: "Instead of your [former] shame you shall have a twofold recompense." The word *recompense* means "reward," or "payment for past hurts." Recompense reminds me of the word *compensation*. When I think of workman's compensation, I think of payment made to a person who has been injured on a job. Always remember, if we get hurt while working for God, He takes care of us; He "pays" us, so to speak. We are not on the world's payroll; God is watching over us. If someone comes against us, if someone hurts us, if someone rejects us, if someone wounds us, we need to keep serving God and doing right, and He will make sure we get what we deserve in the end.

Realizing that I did not have to try to collect from people who hurt me was life-changing for me. The truth is, they could not pay me. They could not give me back what they took from me, but God can always give you more than people take from you.

We find another promise of reward in Joel: "And I will restore or replace for you the years that the locust has eaten—the hopping locust, the stripping locust, and the crawling locust, My great army which I sent among you. And *you shall eat in plenty and be satisfied* and praise the name of the Lord, your God, Who has dealt wondrously with you. And My people shall never be put to shame" (Joel 2:25–26 emphasis mine).

Note the words I have italicized: "you shall eat in plenty and be satisfied." This part of the promise means so much to me because I spent so many years dissatisfied and discontent. No matter what I had, I wasn't satisfied. No matter what anybody did for me, I wasn't satisfied. No matter what I accomplished, I was not satisfied. Why? Because only God can satisfy.

Whatever you have lost in your life, He will restore. That's a promise. He will repay what has been stolen from you. As you trust Him, He will make sure you "shall eat in plenty and be satisfied and praise the name of the Lord."

YOU'RE ON YOUR WAY

There is a reason you chose to read this book. I suspect something about its title, *Never Give Up!*, caught your attention. Maybe you have lived your entire life with a hope, a dream, or a goal you feel is so important it is worth never giving up on; you will make any sacrifice to see that dream come true or fight your way through any hardship to reach it. Perhaps you are facing a situation right now and you know the only way to survive it is to never give up. Maybe you have given up on something in the past and want to make sure you do not give up again.

Whatever the reason, I want to personally encourage you one more time to *never give up.* I also want to make sure you know God often moves suddenly when people have pressed in and pressed on for years, refusing to give up. Don't despair, because your breakthrough may "suddenly" come today, and if not today, then perhaps tomorrow or the next day. He hears every prayer you have ever prayed about your struggles, and He sees the commitment you demonstrate and watches you as you overcome adversity in pursuit of all He has for you. I believe there will be moments and seasons in which He will suddenly give you the provision you need, open the doors of opportunity you are waiting for, give you the ideas you are missing, align the relationships that need to come together, or do whatever you are longing for Him to do in your life. It will happen, and it may seem to be a "suddenly" for you.

I believe most of the time, only the *results* come suddenly. Behind every seemingly sudden victory, breakthrough, great opportunity, achievement, or blessing lies a degree of faithful perseverance and determination known only to those who have done the pressing.

> *Most of the time, only the* results *come suddenly.*

You may have to wait much longer than you'd like before you finally enjoy the satisfaction of a goal accomplished or a desire fulfilled. Waiting—and waiting patiently and expectantly—are part of never giving up. Whatever you are believing God to bring to pass in your life, be patient, enjoy the journey, and refuse to give up.

You may not be able to change your circumstances, but you can be determined to wait on God and trust Him to do it. You may have to wait longer than you thought or hoped you would, but God will not be late. While you wait, you can be confident God will come through for you. When He does, you will be so glad you persevered.

God has a wonderful, unique plan for you, and I encourage you to be determined to see the fullness of that plan come to pass in your life. When life seems difficult and you are tempted to quit, remember those who have gone before you. Remember those who never gave up and eventually enjoyed the rewards of their faith and hope.

Will you decide right now that no matter what happens in life, you will never give up? The choice is up to you, but I assure you, whatever you have to overcome to reach your goals and enjoy the success God has for you will be worth the effort.

Be determined; be committed; be patient; and be diligent in every area of your life—and whatever you do, never give up!

PRAYER OF SALVATION

The most important relationship of your life is a personal relationship with Jesus Christ. If you would like to receive Him as your Lord and Savior, and enter into the greatest relationship you have ever known, please pray the prayer below:

Father,

You loved the world so much You gave Your only begotten Son to die for our sins so that whoever believes in Him will not perish but have eternal life.

Your Word says we are saved by grace through faith as a gift from You. There is nothing we can do to earn salvation.

I believe and confess with my mouth that Jesus Christ is Your Son, the Savior of the world. I believe He died on the cross for me and bore all of my sins, paying the price for them.

I believe in my heart that You raised Jesus from the dead and that He is alive today.

I am a sinner; I am sorry for my sins; and I ask You to forgive me. By faith I receive Jesus Christ now as my Lord and Savior. I believe that I am saved and will spend eternity with You! Thank You, Father. I am so grateful! In Jesus' name, Amen.

APPENDIX

STORIES OF INDIVIDUALS WHO NEVER GAVE UP

Introduction

Chapter 1

Chapter 2

Chapter 3

Chapter 4

Chapter 5

Chapter 6

Chapter 7

Chapter 8

Chapter 9

Chapter 10

ABOUT THE AUTHOR

JOYCE MEYER is one of the world's leading practical Bible teachers. A #1 *New York Times* best-selling author, she has written more than seventy inspirational books, including *The Confident Woman, I Dare You,* the entire *Battlefield of the Mind* family of books, her first venture into fiction with *The Penny,* and many others. She has also released thousands of audio teachings as well as a complete video library. Joyce's *Enjoying Everyday Life*® radio and television programs are broadcast around the world, and she travels extensively conducting conferences. Joyce and her husband, Dave, are the parents of four grown children and make their home in St. Louis, Missouri.

JOYCE MEYER MINISTRIES
U.S. & FOREIGN OFFICE ADDRESSES

Joyce Meyer Ministries
P.O. Box 655
Fenton, MO 63026
USA
(636) 349-0303
www.joycemeyer.org

Joyce Meyer Ministries—Canada
P.O. Box 7700
Vancouver, BC V6B 4E2
Canada
1-800-868-1002

Joyce Meyer Ministries—Australia
Locked Bag 77
Mansfield Delivery Centre
Queensland 4122
Australia
(07) 3349 1200

Joyce Meyer Ministries—England
P.O. Box 1549
Windsor SL4 1GT
United Kingdom
01753 831102

Joyce Meyer Ministries—South Africa
P.O. Box 5
Cape Town 8000
South Africa
(27) 21-701-1056

Worry is a down payment on a problem
you may never have.
Is it working?

I have determined I'm going
to live in peace

Worry causes illness, etc
"I am not going to live in worry.
torment one's selve with
disturbing thoughts; to feel
uneasy

Matthew 6

Love Life
Sept 15-17
St. Louis

Do what you can do — God will do what you can't do

Why, God, Why?
The Word, the Name, the Blood
Tell Them I Love Them
Peace
If Not for the Grace of God*

* Study Guide available for this title.

selfcontrol - power of words

1. line your mouth up w/ the word of God
   Never/never/never/ say bad things
   about yourself. Do not say
   unkind things about yourself
   I'm not weird - I'm unique

Maligni — Mol a ki

2. Be careful how you talk about God.
   Do not talk unkindly about
   God. He's good. What ever
   is wrong w/ world

3 Be careful how you talk
   people
   about others. Use self control
   "Cover your friends." Use self
   control. Gen. 9 — love covers
   a multitude of sins.

4. Be careful how you talk during
   your time of trials. "So he
   opened not his mouth"

Collosians
3   set your mind & keep it set.
    start a project — finish it.
Proverbs   self control.
25:28   make a plan